Warrior Mindset

Avi Meir Zaslavsky, Theodore Green

Disclaimer

You are about to embark on a transformative journey with "Warrior Mindset." But before you do, it is important to understand the context, limitations, and responsibilities associated with the content provided in this book.

You are ultimately responsible for your results. The strategies outlined in this book are designed to help you develop a warrior mindset, but they are not a guaranteed one-size-fits-all solution. Your success will depend on your commitment, mindset, and the specific circumstances of your life.

The warrior mindset is about more than just being tough. It is about developing a deep inner strength, resilience, and courage that enables you to face any challenge head-on. The strategies outlined in this book are diverse and can be adapted to fit your individual needs and preferences. Experiment and find what works best for you.

The authors of this book are dedicated researchers and writers but not licensed therapists or mental health professionals. The content is based on extensive research and understanding, but it is important to consult qualified professionals, especially concerning mental health issues. This book does not replace the expertise provided by trained psychologists, counselors, or medical practitioners.

Throughout this book, there might be references to external websites, books, and resources. These references are meant for informational purposes and convenience only. The authors do not endorse or take responsibility for the content, accuracy, or reliability of external sources. Please use your discretion and verify the credibility of any external resources before using them.

This book might reference cultural or historical examples to illustrate certain points. It is important to approach these examples with cultural sensitivity and understanding. This book does not endorse or condone any form of violence, discrimination, or harm towards

WARRIOR MINDSET

others. The warrior spirit, as discussed in this book, is about personal growth, resilience, and fearlessness in the face of challenges, not aggression or harm.

You are encouraged to provide feedback and comments and engage in discussions related to this book. However, all interactions must be conducted respectfully and in adherence to ethical guidelines. The author reserves the right to moderate and remove any inappropriate or offensive content.

By proceeding to read this book, you acknowledge and accept the terms outlined in this disclaimer. Engaging with its content implies your understanding of these boundaries and your commitment to using the information responsibly and ethically.

Contents

Introduction

A warrior mindset is a state of mind that allows one to face challenges and adversity with courage, strength, and determination. It is characterized by resilience, perseverance, and a never-give-up attitude.

There are many benefits of having a warrior mindset. First, it allows you to overcome challenges more easily. When you have a warrior mindset, you are not afraid of challenges. You see them as opportunities to grow and learn.

Second, a warrior mindset allows you to achieve your goals. With a warrior mindset, you are focused and determined to achieve your goals. You do not let anything or anyone stand in your way.

Third, a warrior mindset helps you make better decisions. When you have a warrior mindset, you think clearly and rationally under pressure, and you are not swayed by emotions or fear.

Fourth, a warrior mindset helps you to be more resilient in the face of adversity. With a warrior mindset, you can bounce back from setbacks and failures. You do not give up easily.

Fifth, a warrior mindset helps you to be more successful in all areas of life. A warrior mindset is not just about overcoming challenges and achieving goals. It is also about living a life that is true to yourself and your values.

This book will teach you how to develop a warrior mindset. You will learn how to overcome your fears, develop mental toughness, and build resilience. You will also learn how to apply the warrior mindset to business, life, and relationships.

Chapter 1: The Warrior Mindset

G reat people often have a warrior mindset. This mindset means being strong, not giving up, and not fearing challenges. It's important for success in life and work. It's like armor that protects you from self-doubt, fear, and problems.

In this chapter, we will learn more about the warrior mindset. We will look at old and new ideas to find the secrets that help warriors win. By the end, you will know what a warrior mindset is and how to have it in all parts of your life. Are you ready to become a fearless warrior? Let's start the journey.

What is the Warrior Mindset?

Imagine yourself standing on a battlefield, facing a formidable opponent. Your heart is pounding in your chest, your palms are sweaty, and your mind is racing. But you know that you must overcome your fear and fight. You take a deep breath, center yourself, and draw on your inner strength. You are a warrior.

The warrior mindset is not just for soldiers on a battlefield. It is a way of thinking and living that can help you overcome any challenge, big or small. It is a mindset of courage, strength, determination, and resilience.

When you embrace the warrior mindset, you see challenges as opportunities for growth and learning. You understand that failure is not a sign of weakness but a stepping stone to success. You are constantly striving to improve yourself and achieve your goals.

Courage, resilience, discipline, and an unyielding spirit are the foundation of your psychological makeup. This mindset isn't merely a collection of thoughts; it's a deeply ingrained way of thinking and acting. You possess a profound understanding of your goals, an unshakeable faith in your abilities, and an unwavering dedication to your endeavors.

Challenges are not adversaries to be feared; they are puzzles to be solved and lessons to be learned. When faced with a daunting task, you dissect the challenge, break it into manageable parts, and diligently tackle each component. Each small victory fuels your confidence, propelling you closer to your goal. You persist even when the going gets tough, reminding yourself that every setback is a setup for a comeback.

Resilience is a cornerstone of your warrior mindset. You don't avoid failure; you learn to bounce back stronger after each fall. Life's adversities, be it a personal loss or a professional setback, are not the end of your journey; they are detours. You understand that setbacks are temporary and you can overcome any hurdle with perseverance. When faced with failure, you analyze the situation, identify areas for improvement, and bounce back with renewed vigor. Every failure becomes a valuable lesson, guiding you toward a better version of yourself.

Discipline is the guiding principle that keeps your warrior mindset on track. It's the daily commitment to your goals, the unwavering focus on the path ahead. You make choices that align with your objectives, even when taking the path of least resistance is easier. You wake up early to work on your passion, resist distractions, and stay committed to your journey. Discipline transforms fleeting motivation into lasting habits, ensuring you steadily progress toward your goals.

Courage is the heartbeat of your warrior mindset. It's not the absence of fear but the ability to act despite it. Every step you take, every challenge you face, requires courage. It's the bravery to face uncertainties, to step into the unknown, and to confront your deepest fears. Courage empowers you to take risks, knowing that failure is not the end but a stepping stone to success. With each courageous act, your confidence grows, reinforcing the warrior mindset and propelling you toward even greater achievements.

You embrace setbacks as opportunities for recalibration. When faced with a setback, you assess the situation objectively, identify the root causes, and adjust your approach. This adaptability ensures that setbacks do not derail your progress but serve as valuable feedback. It's a continuous process of learning and refining your strategies, ensuring you grow stronger with every challenge.

The warrior mindset isn't reserved for a select few; it's a choice available to everyone. It starts with a shift in perspective, viewing challenges not as threats but as gateways to personal evolution. Embracing the warrior mindset empowers you to navigate life's complexities with grace and resilience. It's a journey of self-discovery and growth, where every challenge becomes an opportunity to unleash your inner warrior and conquer the battlefield of life.

Here are some examples of how the warrior mindset can be applied in everyday life:

- **At work:** A warrior mindset can help you to set ambitious goals, overcome challenges, and persevere in the face of setbacks. For example, if you are working on a difficult project, a warrior mindset will help you to stay focused, motivated, and resilient, even when things get tough.

- **In relationships:** A warrior mindset can help you to communicate effectively, resolve conflict, and build strong and lasting relationships. For example, suppose you are facing a challenge in your relationship. In that case, a warrior mindset will help you confront the issue head-on, communicate openly and honestly with your partner, and work together to find a solution.

- **In your personal life:** A warrior mindset can help you to achieve your fitness goals, learn new skills, and live a more fulfilling and meaningful life. For example, if you are trying to lose weight, a warrior mindset will help you to stay disciplined and motivated, even when you feel like giving up.

The Benefits of a Warrior Mindset

You are a warrior. You have a resilient spirit and an indomitable drive. You are not afraid to face challenges head-on and always rise stronger from setbacks. You live with integrity and authenticity, and you are committed to making a positive impact on the world.

A warrior mindset is a powerful tool for achieving goals in all areas of life. It equips you with the mental and emotional resilience to overcome obstacles, build meaningful relationships, and live a fulfilling life. Here are some of the benefits of having a warrior mindset:

1. Mental resilience: A warrior mindset allows you to rebound from failures stronger than before. You don't see setbacks as defeats; instead, you view them as opportunities to learn and grow. This mental toughness is essential for success in any field, whether business, relationships, or personal development.

2. Emotional intelligence: A warrior mindset nurtures your ability to understand and manage your own emotions, as well as the emotions of others. This emotional intelligence helps you build strong relationships, navigate difficult situations, and remain composed under pressure.

3. Sense of purpose: A warrior mindset gives you a clear sense of purpose and direction. You know what you want to achieve in life and are unwavering in your commitment to your goals. This sense of purpose fuels your actions and motivates you to persevere, even when things get tough.

4. Fearlessness: Warriors are not afraid to take risks and step outside their comfort zone. They understand that failure is part of the journey and are willing to learn from their mistakes. This fearlessness allows them to achieve great things, even in adversity.

5. Resilience: Warriors are incredibly resilient. They don't let setbacks deter them; instead, they use them as fuel to push forward. When they fall, they get back up stronger than before. This resilience is essential for success in any area of life, as it allows you to overcome challenges and achieve your goals, no matter what.

Living with a warrior mindset leads to a more fulfilling life. You align your actions with your values and beliefs, living authentically and fearlessly. You stand up for your beliefs, even when it's difficult. You radiate authenticity, inspiring others to embrace their true selves and live their lives with integrity.

Furthermore, a warrior mindset equips you to make a positive impact on the world. You harness your strengths and talents to contribute meaningfully to society. Whether through acts of kindness, leadership, or innovation, you become a beacon of inspiration for others. Your positive energy is contagious, uplifting those around you and creating a ripple effect of goodness.

You are a warrior. You have the power to achieve great things. Embrace your warrior mindset and live your life to the fullest.

Here is a personal story that illustrates the benefits of a warrior mindset:

I used to be timid. I was afraid to speak up in class or at social gatherings. I also had a hard time believing in myself and my abilities. One day, I decided that I wanted to change my life. I wanted to become more confident and assertive. I wanted to be able to go after my goals without fear.

I started by reading books and articles about developing a warrior mindset. I also started working with a coach who helped me to identify my values and beliefs, set clear goals, and develop a plan to achieve them.

It wasn't easy, but I developed a warrior mindset over time. I became more confident and assertive. I also started to achieve my goals. I started my own business and have now built a successful career. I am still a work in progress, but I am grateful for the warrior mindset that I have developed. It has helped me to live a more fulfilling life and to make a positive impact on the world.

How to Know if You Have a Warrior Mindset

Having a warrior mindset means confronting challenges with courage, standing tall in the face of adversity, and bouncing back from failures. It's not about the absence of fear but the ability to act despite it. Reflect on your reactions to challenges and setbacks; they are windows into your mindset. A warrior mindset isn't void of doubts; it's the tenacity to push forward despite uncertainties. If you find yourself embracing challenges, learning from failures, and persisting with unwavering determination, you likely have the foundation of a warrior mindset.

To recognize if you possess a warrior mindset, delve into your inner self. Ask yourself if you confront challenges head-on, if you persist in your goals, and if setbacks strengthen your resolve. Consider if you align your actions with your values and use your strengths to create a positive impact. Your honest answers to these questions unveil the essence of your mindset. If you respond with a resounding yes to most, you're already nurturing a warrior spirit within you.

However, fret not if you hesitated or answered no to some questions. Developing a warrior mindset is a journey, not an instant destination. It begins with acknowledging your fears and uncertainties and then mustering the courage to face them. Remember, every warrior has faced moments of doubt; what sets them apart is their determination to persist. Think of it as building a mental muscle; the more you exercise it, the stronger it becomes.

Consider this: a skilled archer didn't master the art overnight. It took practice, patience, and the will to learn from missed shots. Similarly, cultivating a warrior mindset involves continuous learning and adaptation. Embrace challenges as opportunities to refine your skills and outlook. With each obstacle, you gain experience, enhancing your ability to navigate future hurdles. Every setback becomes a stepping stone, propelling you toward your goals.

Moreover, having a warrior mindset isn't a solitary endeavor. Surround yourself with like-minded individuals who inspire and challenge you. Engage with a supportive community that understands the value of resilience and determination. Together, you can learn from each other's experiences and reinforce your warrior spirit. Remember, warriors rise stronger when they stand united, drawing strength from their shared determination.

Here are some signs that you have a warrior mindset:

- You confront challenges head-on. You don't shy away from difficult tasks or situations. Instead, you embrace them as opportunities for growth and development.

- You're persistent in pursuit of your goals. No matter how many setbacks you face, you never give up on your dreams.

- You bounce back from setbacks and failures quickly. You don't let them define you or derail your progress. Instead, you learn from your mistakes and move on.

- You live your life in accordance with your values and beliefs. You stand up for what you believe in, even when it's unpopular.

- You use your strengths and talents to make a difference in the world. You're committed to using your gifts to help others and make the world a better place.

Here are some examples of how a warrior mindset might manifest in real life:

- A student who fails a test doesn't give up on their studies. Instead, they identify their areas of weakness and work hard to improve.

- An athlete who is injured during training doesn't let it derail their career. Instead, they focus on their rehabilitation and come back stronger than ever.

- An entrepreneur who faces financial setbacks doesn't throw in the towel. Instead, they pivot their business model and keep trying.

- A social activist who faces opposition to their cause doesn't give up fighting. Instead, they continue to speak out for what they believe in.

Developing Your Warrior Mindset

Self-reflection is a powerful tool for growth. Take time each day to reflect on your thoughts, actions, and emotions. What went well? What could have gone better? What lessons can you learn from your experiences? This introspection will help you refine your mindset and develop the resilience and adaptability of a warrior.

Gratitude is another essential ingredient for a warrior mindset. When you focus on the good things in your life, big or small, you cultivate a positive outlook and empower yourself to face challenges with hope. Take a few minutes each morning to appreciate the people, places, and things you're grateful for. Even if it's just something simple like a warm cup of coffee or a beautiful sunrise, gratitude can uplift your spirit and strengthen your resolve.

Mindfulness and meditation are powerful practices for developing mental resilience. When you train your mind to stay focused on the present moment, you learn to remain calm and centered even in the midst of chaos. This mental clarity is essential for making sound decisions and navigating challenges with a warrior's poise. Imagine a serene lake; even when ripples disturb its surface, the depths remain undisturbed. This is the unwavering mental strength you'll cultivate through mindfulness and meditation.

A warrior's power is not just physical; it also stems from empathy and compassion. Take the time to understand the perspectives of others, both their struggles and triumphs. When you see the world through their eyes, you develop a deeper appreciation for the human experience and build stronger relationships. This compassion also nurtures your inner strength, giving you the courage to stand up for what's right and positively impact the world.

Your physical health is also essential for supporting your mental fortitude. Eat a balanced diet, get regular exercise, and get enough sleep. A healthy body gives you the energy and stamina you need to persevere in adversity. Just as a sturdy castle needs a strong foundation, your warrior mindset requires a healthy body to thrive.

Fear is a natural part of life, but warriors don't let it hold them back. When you face your fears head-on, you build courage and confidence. This fearless approach to life allows you to seize opportunities and achieve your goals, even when others doubt you. Imagine standing at the cliff's edge; the fear of falling is real, but your courage propels you to leap. This is the fearless spirit of a warrior.

Finally, remember that your warrior mindset is a journey, not a destination. Embrace change and be open to new experiences. Life's twists and turns are opportunities to sharpen your mindset further and deepen your understanding of yourself. Like a river carving its path through rugged terrain, your warrior mindset will mold you into a resilient, courageous, and determined individual, ready to conquer any obstacle in your way.

Chapter 2: The Warrior's Aim

L ife is a battlefield, and every warrior needs a target. Your purpose fuels you and drives you forward. Your goals guide you and keep you focused. This chapter will explore how to define your purpose, set goals aligned with that purpose, create a strategic plan, and stay focused and motivated. We will also dive deeper into the mental toughness, emotional resilience, and unwavering courage essential for every fearless warrior.

By the end of this chapter, you will have not only defined your purpose and set fearless goals, but you will also have the tools and mindset to achieve them.

Defining Your Purpose

Imagine a ship without a sail. It will be lost at sea, drifting aimlessly in the wind and current, with no destination or purpose. The same is true of a warrior without a purpose. They wander through life, lost and directionless. They may be strong and skilled, but they will never reach their full potential without a purpose to drive them.

To develop a warrior mindset, you must first define your purpose. What is it that you want to achieve in life? What is your legacy? Once you know your purpose, you can start setting goals and developing a plan to achieve them.

I have always been passionate about helping others. I volunteered at a local soup kitchen and homeless shelter when I was younger. As I got older, I realized I could make a bigger difference by starting businesses and helping others become better entrepreneurs. I am now a marketer and entrepreneur and forever grateful for the opportunity to inspire and empower others to follow their passion. I know I am making a difference in their lives, which is my purpose.

This purpose drives me every day. It motivates me to be the best entrepreneur and business coach and reminds me of why I do this. I encourage you to take some time to define your purpose and develop a statement of purpose. It is a powerful tool to help you achieve your goals and live your best life.

Here are some questions you can ask yourself to help you define your purpose:

- What are my passions? What do I love to do?

- What am I good at? What skills and talents do I have?

- What do I want to make a difference in the world? What problems do I want to solve?

- What kind of legacy do I want to leave behind? How do I want to be remembered?

Take some time to reflect on these questions and write down your answers. The more specific you can be, the better. Once you understand your purpose well, you can start developing a statement of purpose. This statement should be concise and inspiring. It should also be something that you can refer back to when you need motivation.

Here is an example of a statement of purpose: "My purpose is to inspire and empower others to achieve their goals and live their best lives."

This statement is concise, inspiring, and specific. It also reflects the writer's passions (helping others) and their skills and talents (inspiring and empowering others).

Once you have a statement of purpose, you can develop goals and a plan to achieve them. Your goals should be aligned with your purpose, and they should be challenging but achievable. Break down your goals into smaller, more manageable steps. This will make them seem less daunting and more achievable.

As you work towards your goals, you will inevitably face challenges. This is where your warrior mindset will come in. Remember your purpose and why you are doing this. Remember that you are strong and capable. And never give up.

Setting Goals That Align with Your Purpose

What is your guiding star? What empowers you to rise each morning and pursue your goals? Once you know your purpose, craft SMART goals that resonate deeply with your essence. For example, if your purpose is to inspire young minds, your goals could involve becoming a certified teacher, developing innovative educational resources, or mentoring aspiring students. Your goals are not mere objectives but essential components of your warrior blueprint.

Warriors don't shy away from challenges; they see them as doors to growth and platforms to enhance their skills. When faced with a daunting task, such as educating a diverse group of students, don't feel overwhelmed. Instead, view this challenge as an opportunity to innovate your teaching methods, cater to individual needs, and enrich your skills. They are necessary for personal development.

Warriors don't back down easily. They persist in the face of set-backs, learning from their experiences and adapting their approach. When your lesson plan doesn't go as planned, don't let it derail you. The warrior mindset nudges you to reevaluate, learn, and adapt. It's this persistent spirit that transforms setbacks into setups for future success. Persevere, not just because you have to, but because your warrior identity demands it.

Life is unpredictable, and challenges are bound to appear unex-pectedly. Resilience is your shield, guarding you against the arrows of disappointment and failure. When external circumstances threaten to derail your educational initiatives, don't give up. Resilience, in the warrior's context, means pivoting your strategies, finding alternate routes, and standing firm against the storm. Bounce back stronger af-ter every setback, your spirit unbroken and determination unyielding.

Adopting the warrior mindset doesn't mean denying fear; it means confronting it head-on. Warriors acknowledge their fears but don't let fear dictate their actions. When fear creeps in before a crucial presentation or a challenging classroom situation, confront it with courage. Remember, fear is a natural emotion. Don't let it paralyze you. This courage, rooted in the warrior mindset, propels you to face challenges boldly, transforming fear into a catalyst for personal and professional growth.

Now that you understand your purpose well, it's time to start setting goals that will help you achieve it. Your goals should be SMART, meaning they should be specific, measurable, achievable, relevant, and time-bound.

Here's what each of those criteria means:

- **Specific:** Your goals should be as specific as possible. The more specific you are, the easier it will be to track your progress and stay motivated. For example, instead of setting a goal to "get in shape," set a goal to "lose 10 pounds in 3 months" or "run a 5K race in 6 months."

- **Measurable:** Your goals should be measurable so that you can track your progress and see how close you are to achieving them. For example, instead of setting a goal to "learn more about photography," set a goal to "take 100 photos this month" or "complete a beginner photography course in 2 months."

- **Achievable:** Your goals should be achievable but not too easy. If your goals are too easy, you won't be challenged and feel a sense of accomplishment when you achieve them. On the other hand, if your goals are too difficult, you may become discouraged and give up.

- **Relevant:** Your goals should be relevant to your purpose. Make sure that each one will help you move closer to achieving your overall purpose.

- **Time-bound:** Your goals should have a deadline. This will help you stay focused and motivated. For example, instead of setting a goal to "write a book," set a goal to "write one chapter of my book each week for the next year."

Creating a Plan to Achieve Your Goals

You are a warrior. You have set your sights on a goal and are determined to achieve it. But how do you get from where you are now to where you want to be?

The first step is to create a plan. This may seem daunting, but it doesn't have to be. Just think of it as a roadmap to help you stay on track and progress towards your goal. Here are some tips for creating a strategic plan to achieve your goals:

- Define your goals clearly and specifically. What exactly do you want to achieve? What will it look like when you have reached your goal?

- Break down your goals into smaller, more manageable steps. Once you clearly understand your overall goal, break it down into smaller, more manageable steps. This will make your goal seem less daunting and more achievable.

- Set realistic deadlines for each step. Don't try to do too much too soon. Set realistic deadlines for each step of your plan, and give yourself enough time to complete each step successfully.

- Identify the resources and support you need. What will you need to achieve your goal? This could include time, money, tools, training, or mentorship.

- Anticipate and plan for obstacles. No plan is complete without considering potential obstacles. Think about what could go wrong and how you will deal with it if it does.

- Be flexible and adaptable. Things don't always go according to plan. Be prepared to adjust your plan as needed to stay on track toward your goal.

Remember, you are a warrior. You have the strength, courage, and determination to achieve your goals. Just create a strategic plan, stay on track, and never give up!

Staying Focused and Motivated

Imagine yourself as a warrior, standing on the battlefield of life, ready to face any challenge that comes your way. Your armor gleams in the sunlight, your sword is sharp, and your mind is clear. You are ready for anything.

But to be a successful warrior, you need more than physical strength and skill. You also need to be mentally focused and motivated. You need to stay on track, even when things get tough. This is where the warrior's discipline comes in.

The warrior's discipline is a set of practices and habits that help one stay focused and motivated, even in the face of adversity. It is a way of training one's mind to be strong and resilient. Here are some specific tips to help you stay focused and motivated:

1. Establish daily rituals that reinforce your commitment to your goals. Just as a warrior trains their body and mind daily, you must develop daily rituals supporting your goals. These rituals could include:

- Meditation: Meditation helps to center your mind and focus on your intentions.

- Exercise: Exercise releases endorphins, which boost mood and energy levels.

- Journaling: Journaling allows you to reflect on your progress, identify areas for improvement, and stay motivated.

- Reading: Reading books and articles related to your goals can help you stay informed and inspired.

- Goal setting: Take time each day to review your goals and plan how to achieve them.

2. Surround yourself with a supportive community. The people you spend time with significantly impact your mindset and motivation. Surround yourself with individuals who share your vision and

aspirations and who will lift you and encourage you to persevere. This could include family, friends, mentors, or a professional network.

3. Learn to say no. It is important to be selective about how you spend your time and energy. Don't be afraid to say no to commitments and requests that do not align with your goals.

4. Celebrate your successes. It is important to acknowledge and celebrate your accomplishments, no matter how small they may seem. This will help you stay motivated and on track toward your ultimate goals.

Imagine yourself as a warrior. You are strong, disciplined, and committed to achieving your goals. You have a clear vision of what you want to achieve and are not afraid to put in the hard work required to make it happen.

Every morning, you wake up early and perform a series of rituals that reinforce your commitment to your goals. You start with a short meditation to center your mind and focus on your intentions. Then, you go for a run to invigorate your body and boost your energy levels. After your run, you journal about your progress and identify areas for improvement.

After your morning rituals, you are ready to start your day. You are focused, motivated, and determined to achieve your goals. You know there will be challenges along the way, but you are confident you have the discipline and the support system to overcome them.

Throughout the day, you make choices that are aligned with your goals. You say no to commitments that distract you from your path, and you focus your energy on the most important tasks.

At the end of the day, you take some time to reflect on your progress and celebrate your successes. No matter how small your accomplishments may seem, you acknowledge and appreciate them. This helps you stay motivated and on track toward your ultimate goals.

By following these tips, you can develop the warrior mindset necessary to stay focused and motivated amidst life's distractions and challenges. Remember, you are strong, disciplined, and capable of achieving anything you set your mind to.

Chapter 3: The Warrior's Fire

The warrior's fire is fueled by passion and guarded by mental toughness. Without passion, a warrior is like a sword without an edge. Without mental toughness, a warrior is like a castle without walls. As you pursue your dreams, remember that the warrior's fire is not extinguished by adversity; it is strengthened by it. In this chapter, we will explore the warrior's path, which includes mental fortitude, emotional resilience, and unwavering courage. We will also show you how to find your passion, build inner strength, and develop mental toughness. You will learn how to cultivate willpower so strong that it will help you overcome any challenge.

Finding Your Passion

Passion is the fire that burns within you, propelling you forward on your life's journey. It's the beacon that guides you through the darkest of nights, illuminating the path to your destiny. Passion is not simply a hobby or an interest; it's something that runs deep within you, stirring your soul and awakening your spirit. It's something that you're willing to fight for, to sacrifice for, to give your all for.

To discover your passion, you must first dive headfirst into the deep end of your inner world. What makes your heart pound like a drum in your chest? What topics send you into a state of hyperfocus, where you lose track of time, and everything else around you fades away? What are you willing to stay up all night working on, even if you have to drag yourself out of bed the next morning feeling exhausted but exhilarated?

Those are the things that are most likely to spark your passion. When you find something that you're truly passionate about, it's not just something that you enjoy doing. It's something that consumes you, something that you can't get enough of, something that you feel compelled to do, even if no one is paying you or telling you to.

So, how do you discover your passion? Here are a few tips:

1. Pay attention to your emotions. What makes you feel happy, excited, fulfilled, challenged, and engaged? When do you feel most alive? Make a list of these things, and start to explore them more deeply.

2. Reflect on your past experiences. What are some of the things that you've done in your life that you've truly loved? What projects have you worked on that you've been most proud of? What skills and talents do you have that you enjoy using?

3. Experiment with new things. Don't be afraid to try new things and step outside of your comfort zone. The more things you try, the more likely you are to find something that you're passionate about.

- **Talk to people who are passionate about what they do.** Ask them about their work, their hobbies, and their interests. What is it about what they do that they love so much? Their stories may inspire you to find your passion.

Once you have a better understanding of yourself, start exploring different possibilities. Experiment with new activities and hobbies. Try your hand at different skills and trades. The more you experience, the closer you'll get to discovering your true passion.

Don't be afraid to step outside of your comfort zone. It's easy to get stuck in a rut, doing the same things day in and day out. But staying in your comfort zone will only hold you back from reaching your full potential.

Stepping outside your comfort zone is the only way to grow and learn. When you try new things, you challenge yourself to think in new ways and to develop new skills. You also open yourself up to new opportunities and experiences.

Of course, stepping outside of your comfort zone can be scary. It's normal to feel anxious or uncertain when you're doing something new. But it's important to remember that the rewards are worth it.

Finding your passion is not a race. It takes time, self-discovery, and experimentation. Be patient with yourself and enjoy the journey. Once you have found your passion, hold on to it tightly. It is your most powerful weapon. It will give you strength, courage, and determination to overcome any obstacle.

Building Inner Strength

Inner strength is not about physical prowess; it is about the unyielding resolve that defines your resilience, the unwavering spirit that faces adversity head-on, and the quiet power that emanates from within. It is the foundation upon which your warrior spirit flourishes.

Acknowledge your fears and insecurities, not as signs of weakness but as courageous steps toward fortitude. Discover the depth of your inner reservoirs through self-compassion, treating yourself with the same kindness and understanding you would a dear friend. This practice is not a mere gesture but a cornerstone, grounding you in the fertile soil of self-acceptance.

Your inner strength is not a static achievement but a dynamic, ever-evolving process of self-discovery. Continuously explore your own depths, accept your imperfections, and learn from your stumbles. Cultivate a robust sense of self-worth, believing in the vast expanse of your capabilities and your inherent capacity for greatness. This belief becomes the bedrock upon which your inner strength flourishes, providing the foundation for your unwavering determination.

Master your emotions. Do not let them dictate your actions. Instead, navigate the turbulent waters of your feelings with calm and collected composure. In moments of emotional turmoil, your inner strength shines brightest, guiding you through the storm with grace and poise. Develop the art of self-discipline, honing your ability to resist distractions and stay laser-focused on your goals. Discipline becomes the guardian of your inner sanctum, preserving the sanctity of your ambitions.

Embrace challenges as benevolent mentors on your journey. Each challenge is an opportunity, a disguised blessing that beckons you to grow and learn. Do not falter; instead, face challenges with unwavering resolve. In the crucible of adversity, your inner strength is tested and tempered, transforming you into a formidable, unyielding, and steadfast warrior.

Remember, building inner strength is not a destination; it is the essence of your being, a continuous odyssey of self-discovery and self-affirmation. Let your inner strength be the vibrant thread that weaves resilience, courage, and unwavering determination into the very fabric of your existence.

Embrace your vulnerabilities, nurture your self-compassion, and face challenges with a heart brimming with self-belief. As you journey onward, remember that your inner strength is not merely a quality; it is the essence of your warrior spirit, a testament to your indomitable willpower.

Here are a few tips to help you build your inner strength:

1. Cultivate a deep understanding of yourself: The first step to building inner strength is understanding your strengths, weaknesses, values, and beliefs. What are you passionate about? What are your core values? What are your strengths and weaknesses? What are your goals and dreams?

The more you understand yourself, the better equipped you will be to make choices that align with your values and goals. You will also better handle challenges and setbacks because you will know what you stand for and are fighting for.

2. Practice self-compassion: Self-compassion is the foundation of inner strength. It is treating yourself with kindness and understanding, even when you make mistakes or fall short of your expectations.

Self-compassion does not mean condoning your mistakes. It simply means accepting yourself as you are, flaws and all. It means understanding that everyone makes mistakes and that we are all learning and growing. When you practice self-compassion, you are building a strong foundation of self-love and acceptance. This foundation will give you the strength to face challenges, overcome setbacks, and persevere in adversity.

3. Challenge yourself to grow: One of the best ways to build inner strength is to challenge yourself to grow and step outside of your comfort zone. When you challenge yourself, you are forced to confront your fears and insecurities. You are also forced to learn new skills and develop new strengths.

There are many ways to challenge yourself. You could take a class, learn a new skill, start a new hobby, or travel to a new place. You could also volunteer your time to a cause that you care about or challenge yourself to step outside of your comfort zone in your personal life. When you challenge yourself, you build inner strength, expand your horizons, and create new opportunities.

4. Surround yourself with positive people: The people you spend time with can profoundly impact your inner strength. If you are surrounded by negative people who constantly put you down, it will be difficult to build yourself up. On the other hand, if you are surrounded by positive people who support your goals and believe in you, it will be much easier to build your inner strength. Make sure to spend time with people who lift you up and make you feel good about yourself.

5. Practice gratitude: Gratitude is a powerful tool for building inner strength. When you focus on the good things in your life, you shift your focus from the negative to the positive. This can help you develop a more optimistic outlook on life, which can lead to greater inner strength. There are many ways to practice gratitude. You could keep a gratitude journal, write a gratitude letter to someone you care about, or take a few minutes each day to reflect on the things you are grateful for.

Building inner strength takes time and effort, but it is a journey well worth taking. By following the tips above, you can start to build a strong foundation of inner strength that will help you navigate life's challenges and live a fulfilling life.

Developing Mental Toughness

Imagine yourself as a warrior, standing tall and proud in adversity. Your mind is a shield, protecting you from the slings and arrows of life. Your spirit is unbreakable, fueled by a deep sense of self-belief. This is the power of mental toughness.

Mental toughness is not a quality you're born with. It's a skill that's developed through practice, perseverance, and self-discipline. Just as a warrior trains their body to withstand the rigors of battle, you can train your mind to withstand the challenges of life.

Every challenge you encounter is an opportunity to strengthen your mental toughness. When you face adversity, don't see it as an obstacle but as a stepping stone to growth. Embrace the challenge with courage and determination.

As you confront your challenges, be honest with yourself about your limiting beliefs. Are you telling yourself you're not good, smart, or strong enough? Challenge these negative thoughts and replace them with empowering affirmations. For instance, instead of saying, "I'm not a good public speaker," tell yourself, "I'm a capable and confident communicator."

Setting realistic goals is essential for developing mental toughness. When you set goals that are too ambitious, you're setting yourself up for disappointment and frustration. This can lead to negative self-talk, decreased motivation, and a loss of confidence.

On the other hand, setting realistic goals can set you up for success. This can boost your confidence, motivation, and resilience. It can also help you stay focused on your long-term goals, even when things get tough.

If you want to improve your physical fitness:

- Set a goal to exercise for 30 minutes, 3 times a week.

- Set a goal to lose 5 pounds in a month.

- Set a goal to run a 5K race.

If you want to improve your mental health:

- Set a goal to meditate for 10 minutes every day.

- Set a goal to journal for 5 minutes every day.

- Set a goal to get 7-8 hours of sleep each night.

If you want to improve your career:

- Set a goal to learn a new skill.

- Set a goal to network with people in your field.

- Set a goal to apply for 3 jobs per month.

As you pursue your goals, don't be afraid to make mistakes. Everyone makes mistakes; they're a natural part of the learning process. The important thing is to learn from your mistakes and move on.

Fear is a natural human emotion, but it doesn't have to define you. It's okay to be afraid, but don't let your fear paralyze you. Instead, use it as motivation to push yourself beyond your comfort zone. When you're faced with a challenge, ask yourself what the worst that could happen. Is it really that bad? In most cases, the answer is no. Even if you fail, you'll learn from your mistakes and come back stronger. Remember, failure is not the opposite of success; it's a part of success. Every successful person has failed at some point in their journey. It's how you respond to failure that determines your true potential.

Developing mental toughness is a lifelong journey. There will be times when you feel challenged, discouraged, and even defeated. But if you persevere, you will emerge stronger and more resilient.

Cultivating Unbreakable Willpower

Willpower is the unyielding determination that propels you toward your goals, even in the face of temptation and adversity. The fierce fire within you urges you forward when things get tough. To cultivate this unbreakable willpower, focus on self-discipline and self-control.

- Identify your triggers and temptations. What typically derails you from your path? Once you know your triggers, you can develop strategies to either avoid them altogether or overcome them when they arise.

For example, if you're trying to lose weight and your favorite bakery is right on your way home from work, you might want to find a different route home or avoid walking past the bakery altogether. Or, if you're trying to focus on a project but your phone is constantly buzzing with notifications, you might want to put your phone in silent mode or even turn it off altogether.

- **Practice delayed gratification.** This means resisting the urge to give in to immediate rewards in favor of longer-term, more meaningful goals. It's like choosing to study for a test instead of watching your favorite TV show or saving up for a down payment on a house instead of buying the latest gadget. Delayed gratification can be difficult, but it's a powerful way to strengthen your willpower. When you resist temptation, you train your brain to say no to gratification. The more you practice delayed gratification, the easier it will become.

- **Set clear boundaries.** Learn to say no to distractions that derail your focus. This may mean declining invitations from friends, turning off the TV, or closing unnecessary tabs on your computer. Setting boundaries can be challenging, but it's essential for cultivating unbreakable willpower. When you can say no to distractions, you're sending a message to yourself that you're serious about achieving your goals.

- **Envision your goals clearly.** What do you want to achieve, and why? A clear vision of your goals will give you direction and motivation, even when things get tough. Take time to write down your goals and why they're important. Keep this list where you can see it often, such as on your fridge or in your journal. Whenever you feel tempted to give up, remind yourself of your goals and why you're working so hard to achieve them.

- **Make a heartfelt commitment to yourself.** Decide unequivocally that you will achieve your goals, no matter what obstacles stand in your way. This commitment will act as your inner compass, guiding your efforts and determination toward your desired outcomes. When you make a commitment to yourself, you're essentially saying that you believe in yourself and your ability to achieve your goals. This self-belief is essential for cultivating unbreakable willpower.

- **Break down your goals into smaller, more manageable steps.** When faced with a colossal task, it can be daunting and overwhelming. But breaking it down into smaller, more manageable steps makes it much less daunting and more achievable. Think of it like climbing a mountain. If you look at the entire mountain all at once, it may seem impossible to climb. But if you break it down into smaller steps, such as climbing one ledge at a time, it becomes much more doable.

- **Establish a routine.** Having a structured daily plan will help you stay on track and make consistent progress toward your goals. It will also provide you with a sense of stability and normalcy, which can be helpful when you're facing challenges. Your routine doesn't have to be complicated. It can be as simple as setting aside time each day to work on your goals or having a specific time each night to go to bed and wake up. The important thing is to have a plan and stick to it as much as possible.

- **Celebrate your victories.** No matter how small your victories may seem, it's important to celebrate them. Acknowledging your achievements, no matter how small fuels your motivation and reinforces your belief in your abilities. When you achieve a goal, take some time to celebrate. This could be something as simple as treating yourself to a small gift or taking a break to do something you enjoy. Celebrating your victories will help you stay motivated and on track toward your ultimate goals.

Cultivating unbreakable willpower is a journey, not a destination. Developing the strength and determination to overcome challenges and achieve your goals takes time and effort. But if you're willing to put in the work, it's definitely possible.

Remember, you're stronger than you think. You have the power to achieve anything you set your mind to. Embrace your inner warrior spirit and cultivate unbreakable willpower. The world is yours for the taking.

Chapter 4:
The Warrior's
Fearlessness

F earlessness is the most essential quality of a warrior. It is what turns ordinary people into extraordinary beings. Fear is a natural instinct, but warriors must overcome and master it. In this chapter, we will learn about fear, how to conquer it, and how to use it to grow. We will also learn how to develop the unwavering courage that defines a fearless warrior.

For a fearless warrior, fear is not an obstacle. It is a stepping stone, a catalyst, and a proof of their courage. As you read this chapter, remember that fearlessness is not the absence of fear. It is the ability to overcome fear. Every time you understand, overcome, and embrace fear, you come closer to being a fearless warrior.

Understanding the Nature of Fear

Fear is a powerful emotion that can shape our lives. It can motivate us to take action to protect ourselves from danger, but it can also hold us back from living our lives to the fullest. To overcome fear, the first step is to understand it. What is fear? Why do we experience it? And what are the different types of fear?

Fear is a natural human emotion triggered by the perception of danger. It is a complex response that involves both physical and psychological changes. When we are afraid, our bodies release stress hormones such as adrenaline and cortisol. These hormones prepare our bodies to fight or flee the perceived threat.

A range of other emotions, such as anxiety, worry, and panic often accompanies fear. You may also experience physical symptoms such as sweating, trembling, and a racing heart. There are two main types of fear: rational and irrational.

Rational fear is a natural and healthy response to real and imminent danger. It is a powerful motivator that helps us stay safe and avoid harm. Imagine yourself walking home from work late at night. You are in a dark alleyway, and you hear footsteps behind you. Your heart starts to race, and your palms get sweaty. You feel a surge of fear. This is a rational fear. You are in a potentially dangerous situation, and your body is preparing you to respond. Your adrenaline is pumping, and your senses are heightened. You are ready to run if you need to.

Here are some examples of rational fear:

- Fear of heights if you are standing on the edge of a tall cliff

- Fear of fire if you are trapped in a burning building

- Fear of being attacked if you are walking alone in a dark alleyway

- Fear of being hit by a car if you are about to cross a busy street

- Fear of getting sick if you are exposed to a contagious virus

Rational fear motivates us to take steps to protect ourselves. For example, we may avoid walking in dark alleyways or wear a seatbelt when we are driving. We may also take steps to reduce our risk of getting sick, such as washing our hands frequently and getting vaccinated.

Irrational fear is a powerful emotion that can prevent you from living your best life. It's based on an exaggerated or unrealistic threat, and it can be so intense that it prevents you from doing things that you want or need to do. For example, imagine you're afraid of spiders. You know that spiders are mostly harmless, but your fear is so intense that you can't even walk into a room if there's a spider web in the corner. This irrational fear is preventing you from enjoying many simple things in life, like going for a hike or having a picnic in the park.

Or maybe you're afraid of public speaking. You have an excellent idea for a presentation at work, but the thought of standing up in front of a group of people terrifies you. Your fear is so strong that you start to procrastinate on the presentation, and eventually, you miss the deadline. This irrational fear is preventing you from advancing your career and achieving your goals.

Irrational fear can manifest in many different ways. Some people are afraid of specific things, like spiders or public speaking. Others have more general fears, like failure or the unknown. No matter what form it takes, irrational fear can have a significant impact on one's life.

If you want to overcome fear, it is essential to understand the difference between rational and irrational fear. Rational fear is something that we should all have. It is a healthy part of the human condition. Irrational fear, on the other hand, is something that we need to work on overcoming.

Overcoming Your Fears

Fear is a natural human emotion. It can be a powerful motivator, helping us to avoid danger and stay safe. However, fear can also hold us back from living our best lives. It can prevent us from taking risks, pursuing our dreams, and reaching our full potential.

If you want to overcome your fears and live a more fulfilling life, you need to be willing to face them head-on. It's not easy, but it is possible. Here are a few tips to help you on your journey:

1. Identify your fears: The first step to overcoming your fears is to identify them. What are you afraid of? Once you know what you're facing, you can start to develop a plan to overcome it.

2. Challenge your negative thoughts: When we're afraid, our minds often fill up with negative thoughts. We tell ourselves that we're not good enough, that we're going to fail, or that something terrible is going to happen. These negative thoughts can make it difficult to face our fears. That's why it's important to challenge your negative thoughts. Ask yourself if there is any evidence to support them. If not, replace them with more positive thoughts. For example, instead of telling yourself, "I'm going to fail," tell yourself, "I'm going to do my best."

3. Break down your fears into smaller steps: Some fears can be so overwhelming that it seems impossible to face them head-on. That's why it's important to break them down into smaller, more manageable steps.

For example, if you're afraid of public speaking, you could start by practicing your speech in front of a mirror. Once you feel comfortable with that, you could try giving your speech to a small group of friends or family members. Eventually, you can work your way up to speaking in front of larger and larger audiences.

4. Face your fears gradually: Once you have a plan in place, it's time to start facing your fears. But don't try to do too much too soon. Start by facing your smaller fears and gradually work your way up to the bigger ones. It's also important to be patient with yourself. Overcoming fears takes time. Don't get discouraged if you don't see results immediately. Just keep practicing, and eventually, you will reach your goal.

5. Build a support system: Having a support system can be invaluable when you're trying to overcome your fears. Talk to your friends, family, or a therapist about what you're going through. They can offer you encouragement, support, and advice. You can also find support groups for people who are dealing with the same fears as you. These groups can provide a safe and supportive environment where you can share your experiences and learn from others.

6. Use visualization techniques: Visualization techniques can be a powerful way to boost your confidence and prepare yourself to face your fears. To visualize success, close your eyes and imagine yourself facing your fear and coming out on top. Imagine how you will feel when you have overcome your fear. If you do this visualization exercise regularly, you will start to feel more confident in your ability to face your fears.

7. Use positive affirmation: Positive affirmations are another way to boost your confidence and overcome your fears. Repeat positive statements to yourself, such as "I am strong and capable" or "I can overcome my fears." Say these affirmations to yourself regularly, especially when you are feeling afraid. Over time, they will start to sink into your subconscious mind and help you to believe in yourself.

Embracing Fear as a Catalyst for Growth

Facing fear head-on requires courage and a willingness to confront the unknown. Understand that fear is a natural response to change and uncertainty. It's a primal instinct designed to keep you safe, but it can also hold you back if you let it. Acknowledge your fear without judgment, allowing yourself to experience it fully. By accepting its presence, you gain the power to examine it objectively, making it easier to decipher the underlying cause.

Realize that you are not alone in your fears. Every person, regardless of their outward confidence, grapples with fear in various aspects of their lives. This commonality can be a source of strength; knowing that others have faced similar fears and emerged stronger can inspire you. Consider seeking support from friends, family, or even professional counselors who can provide guidance and encouragement.

Another crucial aspect of embracing fear is setting realistic expectations. Understand that growth takes time and effort. You might not conquer your fears overnight, and that's okay. Progress, no matter how small, is still progress. Celebrate your achievements, no matter how minor they seem. Each step forward, no matter how small, brings you closer to overcoming your fears and achieving personal growth.

Moreover, practice self-compassion as you navigate the path of fear. Treat yourself with kindness and understanding, especially when you face setbacks. Avoid self-criticism, as it only reinforces fear and hampers your progress. Remember that self-compassion allows you to bounce back from failures, fostering resilience and strengthening your resolve to face future challenges.

Incorporating fear into your growth journey requires a mindset shift. Instead of viewing fear as an impediment, perceive it as an opportunity for self-discovery and empowerment. Consider fear as a signpost indicating unexplored territories within yourself. These uncharted areas often contain hidden talents, passions, and strengths waiting to be unearthed. Embracing fear as a catalyst for growth opens doors to self-improvement and a deeper understanding of your capabilities.

When I was in high school, I was terrified of public speaking. I would avoid giving presentations at all costs. But I knew that if I wanted to be successful in my career, I would need to learn to overcome my fear. So, I started taking small steps. I started by volunteering to give presentations in class.

It wasn't easy at first, but with each presentation, I got a little bit better. And with each success, my confidence grew. Eventually, I was able to overcome my fear of public speaking altogether. Today, I am a professional speaker and trainer. I love giving presentations and helping others achieve their goals.

If you are struggling with fear, I encourage you to embrace it as a catalyst for growth. It's not always easy, but it's worth it. By facing your fears, you can become a stronger, more resilient, and more confident person.

Developing Unwavering Courage

To develop unwavering courage, you must delve deep within yourself and understand that fear is a natural part of the human experience. Everyone, even the bravest souls, feels fear at some point. Courage is not the absence of fear but the decision to act despite it.

Imagine yourself standing at the edge of a cliff, your heart racing and your palms sweating. Yet, you take that leap of faith anyway. In that moment, you are embracing your courage and demonstrating your resilience and determination to face the unknown.

Courage also involves embracing vulnerability. Allowing yourself to be open to experiences and emotions, even when they scare you, is a testament to your courage. Picture a shy person mustering the strength to speak up in a crowded room. Despite the fear of judgment, they find the strength to share their thoughts. This act of vulnerability is a powerful display of courage.

On your journey to developing unwavering courage, embrace situations that make you uncomfortable. It could be initiating a difficult conversation, pursuing a new career path, or expressing your feelings to someone you care about. Each of these instances requires you to confront your fears head-on and strengthen your courage with every step.

Surrounding yourself with stories of bravery is also crucial. Read about historical figures who faced adversity with unparalleled courage, or listen to stories of contemporary heroes who risked everything for a noble cause. These narratives serve as reminders that courage is not a trait reserved for the extraordinary; it resides within ordinary people just like you. These stories become a beacon of light, guiding you through your challenges and inspiring you to face your fears with unwavering resolve.

Furthermore, unwavering courage is nurtured through self-acceptance and self-compassion. Understand that making mistakes or encountering failures doesn't diminish your courage. It takes courage to admit your flaws, learn from your missteps, and keep moving forward.

Picture a student who, despite failing a test, gathers the strength to study harder and try again. By acknowledging their shortcomings, they demonstrate immense courage and determination to improve. Accept yourself wholly, flaws and all, and recognize that your imperfections don't weaken your courage; they enhance it by teaching you valuable lessons.

Lastly, unwavering courage is sustained by building a support network of people who uplift and encourage you. Surround yourself with individuals who believe in your capabilities and see your potential even when you doubt yourself. These supportive relationships provide a safety net, allowing you to take risks and face challenges, knowing some people have faith in your abilities.

Envision a tightrope walker high above the ground, supported by a safety harness. With this support, they can perform daring feats with confidence, knowing they have a safety net to catch them if they falter. Similarly, a strong support network provides you with the confidence and courage to step outside of your comfort zone and pursue your goals with unwavering determination.

In your pursuit of developing unwavering courage, remember that it's a journey, not a destination. It's about embracing your fears, learning from them, and continuing to move forward despite the uncertainties. With each step, you strengthen your resolve, making courage an integral part of your character.

So, stand tall, acknowledge your fears, and step boldly into the unknown. For it is in those moments of fear that your courage truly shines, illuminating your path with unwavering determination and strength.

Chapter 5: The Warrior's Growth Mindset

The growth mindset is the belief that one's intelligence and abilities can be developed through effort and hard work. People with this mindset believe that they can learn from their mistakes and become better over time.

Warriors need a growth mindset because they are constantly facing challenges and setbacks. They know that they will not always succeed, but they are not afraid to fail. They see failure as an opportunity to learn and grow. In this chapter, we will start a journey of learning about the growth mindset. We will also learn how to develop it and why it is important to accept challenges and failures, as well as the lessons we learn from them.

What is the Growth Mindset?

As a warrior, you know that true strength comes from within. It's not about being physically imposing or invincible; it's about cultivating a mindset that allows you to overcome any challenge. A warrior mindset is one of growth and development. It's about believing in your potential and refusing to give up, no matter what.

One of the most important aspects of a warrior mindset is embracing challenges. Warriors don't shy away from difficult situations; they face them head-on. They understand that challenges are opportunities to learn and grow. When you encounter a challenge, view it as a chance to test your limits and push yourself beyond your comfort zone. Don't be afraid to fail; everyone fails at some point. The important thing is to learn from your mistakes and keep moving forward.

Another critical component of a warrior mindset is resilience. Warriors don't give up easily. They persevere through setbacks and failures, knowing that these experiences make them stronger. When you face a setback, don't let it discourage you. See it as a temporary setback and refocus on your goals. Develop a mantra that you can repeat to yourself when things get tough, such as "I am a warrior, and I will not give up."

Finally, warriors have a growth mindset. They believe that their abilities can be developed through dedication and effort. They don't see their skills as innate or fixed; they view them as fluid and ever-evolving. This mindset allows them to learn and improve constantly. When you want to achieve a goal, break it down into smaller, more manageable steps. Then, focus on taking action one step at a time. As you progress, celebrate your successes, no matter how small they may seem.

How to Develop a Growth Mindset

Imagine a world where you are limitless. Where your potential is boundless and your possibilities are endless. This is the world that awaits you when you cultivate a growth mindset.

A growth mindset is the belief that one can develop one's intelligence and abilities through effort, dedication, and learning. It's a perspective that sees challenges as opportunities for growth and setbacks as temporary setbacks on a journey to mastery.

Developing a growth mindset is like building a sturdy fortress within yourself. It's a foundation of resilience, perseverance, and self-belief. It's a mindset that allows you to embrace challenges head-on, learn from your mistakes, and achieve your goals, no matter how ambitious they may seem.

To embark on this journey of self-discovery and transformation, here are a few fundamental principles to keep in mind:

1. Believe in your capacity to learn and evolve: The first step to cultivating a growth mindset is to believe in yourself. Believe that you are capable of learning and growing, regardless of your past experiences or perceived limitations. Imagine a seed planted within yourself, waiting to sprout and blossom. Nurture this belief with positive affirmations and actions that reinforce your potential.

• **Reframe your challenges as learning opportunities.**

When you face a challenge, don't see it as a setback. Instead, see it as an opportunity to learn and grow. Ask yourself what you can learn from this experience and how you can use that knowledge to improve next time.

- **Celebrate your effort, not just your outcomes.** It's essential to recognize your accomplishments, but it's also important to celebrate the effort you put into achieving them. This will help you to realize that you are capable of great things, even if you don't consistently achieve the outcome you want.

- **Seek out feedback and be open to criticism.** Feedback can be difficult to hear, but it's essential for growth. When someone gives you feedback, listen with an open mind and try to understand their perspective. Then, use that feedback to identify areas where you can improve.

- **Surround yourself with positive people.** The people you spend time with can significantly impact your mindset. Surround yourself with people who believe in you and who support your goals. These people will help you stay motivated and believe in yourself, even when things get tough.

When I was in high school, I was not a very good student. I struggled in math and science, and I often felt discouraged. But one day, my math teacher told me that she believed in me. She said that she could see that I was intelligent and hardworking and that I just needed to believe in myself.

Her words inspired me to change my approach to learning. I started studying harder and asking for help when I needed it. And eventually, I began to see improvement. By the end of the year, I had passed my math class with a good grade. This experience taught me that I am capable of learning and growing, even in areas where I struggle. It also taught me the importance of believing in myself.

2. Embrace challenges as opportunities for growth: Don't be afraid of challenges. Instead, see them as opportunities to grow and learn. When you face a challenge, it means that you are stepping outside of your comfort zone and trying something new. This is where the real magic happens.

When you overcome a challenge, you build resilience and confidence. You learn that you are capable of more than you thought possible. You also expand your horizons and open yourself up to new possibilities.

Setbacks are a normal part of life. Everyone experiences them from time to time. The important thing is not to let them define you. View setbacks as temporary setbacks, not permanent failures. Learn from your mistakes and use them to fuel your growth. What could you have done differently? What did you learn about yourself? What new skills do you need to develop?

Remember, you are not alone. Everyone faces challenges and setbacks in their lives. What matters most is how you choose to respond. Choose to see challenges as opportunities and setbacks as learning experiences. With each challenge you overcome, you become stronger and more resilient.

3. Surround yourself with positivity and inspiration: The people you spend time with have a profound impact on your mindset. If you surround yourself with individuals who embody a growth mindset, their unwavering attitude and approach to challenges will serve as guiding stars, illuminating your path.

Imagine yourself surrounded by people who believe that intelligence and ability can be developed through effort, hard work, and dedication. People who view challenges as opportunities to learn and grow rather than insurmountable obstacles. People who celebrate failures as stepping stones on the road to success.

In the company of such people, you will feel inspired to push yourself beyond your comfort zone and embrace new challenges. You will learn to view setbacks as opportunities to reflect, learn, and grow. You will develop a deeper belief in your potential and a stronger resolve to achieve your goals.

- **Look for mentors and role models.** Identify people in your field or industry who you admire for their success and positive attitude. Reach out to them and see if they would be willing to mentor you or offer guidance.

- **Join clubs and groups that focus on personal growth and development.** There are many online and offline communities where people come together to learn, grow, and support each other. Look for groups that align with your interests and values.

- **Attend workshops and conferences on growth mindset and personal development.** This is a great way to meet like-minded people and learn from experts in the field.

4. Celebrate your successes, no matter how small they may seem: Every success, no matter how small, is a testament to your progress. When you achieve something, no matter how insignificant it may seem, take a moment to celebrate your victory. These small wins may seem like nothing more than building blocks, but they are essential for strengthening the fortress of your growth mindset.

A growth mindset is the belief that your intelligence and abilities can be developed through hard work and dedication. It is the opposite of a fixed mindset, which is the belief that your intelligence and skills are set in stone. People with a growth mindset are more likely to persevere in the face of challenges, take risks, learn from their mistakes, and achieve their goals.

5. Be patient and persistent: Developing a growth mindset takes time and effort, but it is a journey worth taking. It is not a destination but a continuous process of learning and growing. Don't get discouraged if you don't see results immediately. Just keep practicing and persevering, and eventually, you will reach your goals. Every day is an opportunity to reinforce your beliefs, challenge your limits, and celebrate your achievements.

Embracing Challenges and Failure

You are a warrior. You are strong, resilient, and capable of overcoming any challenge that comes your way. But to become the best warrior you can be, you must embrace challenges and failures.

Challenges are like the arrows that point the way to areas in your life that demand growth and development. When confronted with a challenge, don't shrink back. Instead, approach it with curiosity and determination. Dissect the challenge, examining its components and understanding its nuances. For example, if you're faced with a daunting work project, break it down into smaller tasks. This will make the challenge more manageable and allow you to develop your problem-solving abilities.

Failure is another inevitable part of the journey. It's a part of life, and it's a part of the journey to success. No one is perfect, and everyone makes mistakes. The important thing is to learn from our failures and not let them define us.

When you fail, it's easy to feel down. You may feel like a failure yourself. But it's important to remember that failure is not a reflection of your worth. It's simply a sign that you're trying new things and learning from your mistakes. The most successful people in the world have all failed at some point in their lives. But they didn't let their failures stop them. They learned from them and kept moving forward.

Imagine that you're training for a marathon. You've been training hard for months, and you're feeling confident on race day. But then, at the halfway point, you hit the wall. You start to feel cramps in your legs, and you have to slow down to a walk. You're disappointed and frustrated, but you don't give up. You keep going, one step at a time. Eventually, you cross the finish line, and you're overcome with a sense of accomplishment.

Even though you failed to meet your goal of running the entire marathon, you still achieved something remarkable. You persevered through adversity and finished the race. This experience will make you a stronger and more resilient runner. And it will also motivate you to train even harder for your next marathon.

Avoid the trap of fearing failure. It's natural to fear failure. After all, no one wants to fall short of their goals or expectations. But fearing failure can be a self-fulfilling prophecy, preventing you from taking risks and pursuing your dreams.

The good news is that failure is a normal part of life. Even the most accomplished individuals have faced setbacks. Think of famous inventors, artists, and leaders. Thomas Edison tried over 10,000 times to invent the light bulb before he succeeded. Vincent van Gogh's paintings were initially deemed failures, but they're now some of the most celebrated works of art in the world.

Each failure taught Edison and van Gogh something new. It helped them refine their ideas and improve their skills. Ultimately, their failures paved the way for their triumphs.

So, how can you avoid the trap of fearing failure?

Remember that failure is a part of the learning process. Everyone makes mistakes. That's how we learn and grow. Don't be afraid to take risks and try new things, even if you're worried about failing. Reframe your thinking. Instead of seeing failure as a negative experience, view it as an opportunity to learn and improve. What can you take away from this experience? What could you have done differently?

Celebrate your successes. When you achieve a goal, take the time to celebrate your success. This will help you build confidence and resilience.

Embracing failure as an inherent part of the journey liberates you from paralyzing fear, allowing you to experiment, learn, and evolve. Don't let failure define your identity. It's easy to succumb to self-doubt, believing that a single failure signifies incompetence. However, this couldn't be farther from the truth. Failure, in reality, is a testament to your courage to venture into the unknown. Remember, every master was once a beginner. Consider the perseverance of J.K. Rowling, whose initial Harry Potter manuscript was rejected multiple times. Her resilience turned rejection into one of the most beloved literary series worldwide.

Learning from Your Mistakes

Remember that mistakes are not indicators of failure but rather profound lessons in disguise. They serve as insightful guides, illuminating the path toward improvement. The wisdom of a warrior lies in the ability to extract valuable insights from these mistakes and apply them to future endeavors.

When faced with a mistake, take a moment to reflect without self-judgment. Ask yourself: What went wrong? What could you have done differently? What did you learn from this experience? By analyzing your mistakes objectively, you transform them from setbacks into invaluable lessons.

This process aligns with a mindset of continuous improvement, where every mistake becomes an opportunity to refine your skills and knowledge. Imagine a potter shaping clay; with each mistake, the clay becomes smoother, more refined, and more resilient. Similarly, with every mistake, you grow stronger and wiser. Embrace this transformative power of mistakes, for they are the stepping stones toward becoming a better version of yourself. Just as a skilled sailor learns to navigate stormy seas, your ability to learn from mistakes empowers you to navigate life's challenges with grace and determination.

Another crucial aspect of building inner strength is cultivating a positive mindset. Your thoughts have incredible power; they shape your reality and influence your actions. Cultivate positivity by focusing on what you can control and letting go of what you can't. For example, if you face a challenging situation at work, focus on the aspects you can influence, such as your effort and attitude. Accept the things beyond your control, like the opinions of others, and channel your energy into productive endeavors. This positive mindset acts as a shield, protecting you from unnecessary stress and empowering you to face challenges with optimism.

Additionally, building a strong support network is essential on your journey to inner strength. Surround yourself with positive, uplifting individuals who encourage your growth and celebrate your successes. These supportive relationships act as pillars of strength, providing emotional nourishment during tough times. Imagine these relationships as roots grounding a mighty tree; they provide stability and nourishment, allowing you to weather life's storms. Remember, it's not a sign of weakness to seek help or share your struggles. In fact, it takes great courage to open up to others, and doing so strengthens your bond with them, creating a web of resilience that supports you through thick and thin.

Furthermore, practice gratitude as a daily ritual. Take a moment each day to reflect on the things you are thankful for. It could be a small gesture of kindness from a stranger or a moment of joy shared with a loved one. Gratitude shifts your focus from what you lack to what you have, fostering contentment and inner peace. This simple practice enhances your emotional well-being, making you more resilient in the face of challenges. Just as a gardener nurtures plants with water and sunlight, your practice of gratitude nurtures your inner strength, allowing it to flourish and bloom even in adversity.

Always remember to be kind to yourself. Treat yourself with the same compassion and understanding you would offer to a dear friend.

Acknowledge your efforts, no matter how small, and celebrate your progress. Building inner strength is not a race but a gradual, steady journey. Be patient with yourself, and recognize that setbacks are a natural part of growth. Embrace them as opportunities to learn, grow, and become more resilient. Just as a sculptor patiently chisels away to reveal a masterpiece, your journey to inner strength requires patience, dedication, and self-compassion.

Finally, practice mindfulness to stay grounded in the present moment. Often, worries about the future or regrets about the past can cloud your mind, sapping your inner strength. Mindfulness, the practice of being fully present and aware, helps you appreciate the beauty of each moment. It empowers you to respond to challenges with clarity and composure. Imagine your mind as a clear, still pond; mindfulness ensures that even when life's winds blow, the surface remains undisturbed. By cultivating mindfulness, you strengthen your ability to face challenges with a calm and focused mind, enhancing your inner resilience. Remember, building inner strength is a continuous journey, and every step you take brings you closer to the resilient, empowered individual you aspire to be.

Chapter 6: The Warrior's Tools

W arriors have a wide range of tools at their disposal. These tools help them to develop and maintain a warrior mindset. This chapter will discuss five of the most important warrior tools: meditation, visualization, self-talk, affirmations, and gratitude.

Meditation

Meditation is a powerful tool for developing a warrior mindset. It helps to train the mind to focus and be present in the moment, even in the midst of chaos and uncertainty. It also helps to develop self-awareness and compassion, essential qualities for any warrior.

To meditate, find a quiet place where you won't be disturbed. Sit comfortably with your back straight and your feet flat on the floor. Close your eyes and take a few deep breaths. Relax your shoulders and jaw, and allow your body to be at ease.

Now, focus your attention on your breath. Notice the rise and fall of your chest as you inhale and exhale. Don't try to change your breath in any way; observe it. If your mind wanders, gently bring it back to your breath.

As you meditate, imagine yourself as a warrior. See yourself standing tall and strong, with a clear and focused mind. Feel the courage and determination coursing through your veins. You are ready to face any challenge that comes your way.

Continue meditating for as long as you like. When you're ready to finish, take a few deep breaths and open your eyes. Feel the sense of peace and clarity that meditation brings.

Here are some additional tips for meditating as a warrior:

- **Set an intention before you start.** What do you hope to achieve from your meditation? Do you want to develop more focus, courage, or compassion? Once you know your intention, keep it in mind throughout your meditation.

- **Visualize yourself as a warrior.** This will help you to tap into your warrior energy and mindset. You can imagine

yourself in a specific battle scene or simply standing in your
own power.

- **Use affirmations.** Affirmations are positive statements that
  you repeat to yourself to help you achieve your goals. Try
  repeating affirmations such as "I am strong," "I am courageous," or "I am focused" during your meditation.

- **Be patient and persistent.** Meditation takes practice.
  Don't get discouraged if your mind wanders a lot at first. Just
  keep bringing it back to your breath and your intention.

Regular practice of meditation will help you develop a warrior
mindset that will enable you to overcome any challenge and achieve
your goals.

Visualization

Visualization can be your secret weapon as a warrior on your journey to success. It's not just daydreaming; it's a strategic technique that harnesses the incredible power of your imagination. By closing your eyes and delving deep into your mind's eye, you transport yourself into a realm where your goals are not just aspirations but tangible realities. Visualization paints a vivid mental picture where you're not just an observer but an active participant, triumphing over obstacles with unwavering determination.

Create a mental canvas. Imagine a blank canvas within your mind, brimming with infinite possibilities. Here, you craft the scenes of your success story. Visualize yourself at the peak of your achievements, basking in the glory of your hard-earned victories. See the challenges as mere stepping stones, not stumbling blocks. Your mind becomes the artist, filling the canvas with vibrant hues of achievement, resilience, and fulfilment. As you mentally design this masterpiece, you're not just seeing; you're feeling the rush of emotions accompanying triumph – pride, joy, and the satisfaction of reaching your goals.

Overcome obstacles through visualization. Visualization isn't just about picturing the smooth path to success; it's about confronting and overcoming obstacles. Picture hurdles as puzzles waiting to be solved, not roadblocks halting your progress. Visualize yourself devising ingenious solutions, turning setbacks into stepping stones. As you mentally navigate these challenges, your confidence soars. With every obstacle surmounted in your mind, you reinforce the belief that you can overcome anything.

Harness emotional energy. Visualization isn't just a visual exercise; it's an emotional experience. Engage all your senses. Feel the ground beneath your feet, hear the sounds of success, smell the sweet scent of victory. Let these sensory inputs amplify the emotional impact of your visualizations. When you feel the surge of determination and passion, you channel emotional energy into your goals. This emotional charge becomes the driving force behind your actions, propelling you forward with unwavering resolve.

Be consistent. Consistency is the linchpin of effective visualization. Just like a warrior hones their skills through regular practice, visualize your goals daily. Repetition etches these positive images deep into your subconscious, shaping your attitudes and behaviors. The more you immerse yourself in this mental realm of success, the more it becomes an integral part of your psyche. Over time, your mind begins to align with the visions you create, making pursuing your goals a possibility and an inevitability.

Build resilience and confidence. Through visualization, you're programming your mind for success and building resilience and confidence. When you've mentally tackled diverse challenges and emerged victorious, you're fortifying your resilience. This mental resilience translates into real-world tenacity when faced with adversities. Simultaneously, your confidence grows as you visualize yourself achieving your goals repeatedly. Doubts dissipate, making way for a steadfast belief in your abilities. This self-assurance becomes a beacon, guiding your actions and decisions in alignment with your goals.

Embrace your inner warrior. Embrace the warrior within you, armed with physical prowess and the immense power of visualization. With each session, you're sharpening your mental weaponry, becoming adept at navigating the intricate landscapes of your ambitions. Visualization isn't a mere tool; it's your ally in the battle for success. As you embrace this practice wholeheartedly, you're not just seeing your dreams but living them, one vivid mental image at a time.

So, close your eyes, visualize your victories, and let the warrior within you stride confidently toward the future you've designed.

Self-Talk

Self-talk is the inner dialogue that we have with ourselves all day long. It can be either positive or negative, but it has a powerful impact on our thoughts, feelings, and behaviors.

Warriors have positive inner dialogue. They talk to themselves in a supportive and encouraging way. They believe in themselves and their abilities, even when things are tough. To develop a warrior's mindset, you must start by listening to your self-talk. What are you saying to yourself daily? Are you talking to yourself like a friend and supporter or like a critic and bully?

If we constantly criticize ourselves and tell ourselves that we're not good enough, it will be difficult to achieve our goals and live our best lives. Here are some tips for developing a more positive inner dialogue:

- **Become aware of your negative thoughts.** The first step to changing your self-talk is to become aware of your neg-

ative thoughts. Once you're aware of them, you can start to
challenge them.

- **Ask yourself if there's any evidence to support your
  negative thoughts.** Are your negative thoughts based on
  reality, or are they just irrational fears and insecurities? If
  there's no evidence to support your negative thoughts, replace them with more positive and realistic thoughts.

- **Challenge your negative thoughts.** When you have a negative thought, ask yourself if it's true. Is there any other way
  to look at the situation? What would a more positive person
  say to themselves in this situation?

- **Talk to yourself like a friend.** Imagine that your best friend is feeling down and insecure. What would you say to them to cheer them up and boost their confidence? Say those same things to yourself.

- **Repeat positive affirmations.** Positive affirmations are short, positive statements that you can repeat to yourself throughout the day. They can help to reprogram your subconscious mind and train you to think more positively about yourself and your abilities.

I used to be very self-critical. I would constantly beat myself up for my mistakes and shortcomings. No matter what I accomplished, I never felt good enough. One day, I realized that my negative self-talk was holding me back. It was preventing me from taking risks and pursuing my dreams. I decided I needed to change my self-talk to live a happier and more fulfilling life.

I started by paying attention to my negative thoughts. I would write them down in a journal and then challenge them. I would ask myself if there was any evidence to support my negative thoughts and if not, I would replace them with more positive thoughts. I also started talking to myself like a friend. I would tell myself things like, "You're capable and worthy. You're strong and resilient. You can do this."

At first, talking to myself like this felt awkward and fake. But over time, it started to feel more natural. The more I practiced positive self-talk, the better I started to feel about myself and my abilities.

Today, I still have negative thoughts from time to time. But I'm much better at recognizing them and challenging them. I know that I am capable and worthy and can achieve anything I set my mind to. If you're struggling with negative self-talk, I encourage you to start practicing positive self-talk today. It's one of the best things you can do for yourself.

Affirmations

Affirmations are positive statements that you repeat to yourself regularly. They can help reprogram your subconscious mind and create positive changes in your life.

Your subconscious mind is responsible for 95% of your thoughts and behaviors. It constantly scans your environment for evidence to support your beliefs. If you have negative beliefs about yourself, your subconscious mind will find evidence to support those beliefs, which can lead to a self-fulfilling prophecy.

Affirmations can help you to change your negative beliefs into positive ones. When you repeatedly repeat an affirmation to yourself, your subconscious mind eventually starts to believe it. This can positively change your thoughts, behaviors, and emotions.

To use affirmations effectively, follow these steps:

- Choose affirmations that are relevant to your goals. What do you want to achieve in your life? What do you want to improve about yourself? Choose affirmations specific to your goals and that you believe are possible.

- Word your affirmations positively and in the present tense. For example, instead of saying, "I will be confident," say, "I am confident." This will help your subconscious mind believe your affirmation is already true.

- Repeat your affirmations throughout the day. The more you repeat your affirmations, the more likely your subconscious will believe them. You can repeat your affirmations out loud, write them down, or visualize them in your mind.

- Feel the emotion behind your affirmations. As you repeat your affirmations, try to feel the emotion behind them. For example, if you repeat the affirmation, "I am loved and supported," try to feel the feeling of love and support in your body.

- Be patient and consistent. Reprogramming your subconscious mind takes time. Don't get discouraged if you don't see results immediately. Just keep repeating your affirmations, and eventually, you will start to see the changes you want.

Here is an example of how you can use affirmations to reprogram your subconscious mind:

Let's say you have a negative belief about yourself, such as, "I'm not good enough." This belief may be causing you to sabotage your relationships, career, and other areas of your life. To reprogram this negative belief, you can start by repeating the following affirmation to yourself: "I am good enough."

Repeat this affirmation to yourself throughout the day, especially when feeling down or discouraged. As you repeat the affirmation, try to feel the emotion behind it. Imagine yourself feeling confident and worthy. Over time, your subconscious mind will start to believe the affirmation. You will start to see yourself as good enough, and you will start making different life choices.

Gratitude

Gratitude is a powerful tool for warriors. It helps us focus on the good things in our lives, even tough things. When we are grateful, we are more resilient in the face of challenges and more likely to achieve our goals.

Here are a few ways to practice gratitude as a warrior:

- **Start your day with gratitude.** As soon as you wake up, take a few minutes to think about three things that you are grateful for. This could be anything from your warm bed to your loving family to the opportunity to train for another day.

- **Keep a gratitude journal.** Write down three things you are grateful for at the end of each day. This could be big things like your health and loved ones or small things like a delicious meal or a beautiful sunset.

- **Express your gratitude to others.** Let the people in your life know how much you appreciate them. You can do this verbally, in writing, or through small acts of kindness.

- **Be grateful for your challenges.** It may seem strange to be grateful for challenges, but they can help us to grow and become stronger. When we face a challenge, we can learn from it, overcome it, and become more resilient.

Imagine that you are a soldier training for a difficult mission. You are tired, hungry, and sore, and you feel a lot of pressure to succeed. But instead of focusing on the negative, you focus on the positive. You are grateful for the opportunity to train, your health and strength, and the support of your fellow soldiers.

As you train, you visualize yourself completing the mission successfully, overcoming all obstacles, and achieving your goal. This positive visualization helps you stay motivated and focused. When mission day finally arrives, you are prepared. You are confident in your abilities and grateful for the opportunity to serve. You know that you have done everything in your power to prepare and are ready for whatever challenges come your way.

Here are some additional tips for practicing gratitude as a warrior:

- **Be specific.** When you are expressing gratitude, try to be as specific as possible. For example, instead of saying, "I am grateful for my health," say, "I am grateful for my strong muscles and my ability to run long distances."

- **Be mindful.** When you are practicing gratitude, try to be present in the moment and really savor the feeling of gratitude. Take a few deep breaths and allow yourself to feel the positive emotions that arise.

- **Be consistent.** The more you practice gratitude, the easier it will become and the more benefits you will experience. Try to practice gratitude every day, even if it is just for a few minutes.

Positive Habits

Positive habits are essential for developing a warrior mindset. They help us to become more disciplined, focused, and resilient. They also help us to achieve our goals and overcome challenges. Why are positive habits important for a warrior mindset?

Positive habits require discipline to develop and maintain. This discipline can be transferred to other areas of life, such as work, studies, and relationships. Positive habits help you focus on your goals and priorities. They can also help you stay focused in the face of distractions and challenges.

Positive habits can help you bounce back from setbacks and failures. When you have a strong foundation of positive habits, you are less likely to be discouraged by setbacks. Positive habits can also help you achieve your goals and reach your full potential. You feel a sense of accomplishment and empowerment when you consistently progress toward your goals.

Positive habits can help you to challenge yourself and grow. When you push yourself outside your comfort zone, you become stronger, more capable, and more confident.

How to develop positive habits:

- **Identify the habits that you want to change.** The first step to developing positive habits is identifying the ones you want to change. Make a list of your current habits, both good and bad. Once you have a list of your habits, identify the ones you want to change.

- **Set specific goals for yourself.** Once you have identified the habits you want to change, set specific goals. For example, if you want to quit smoking, your goal might be to go one week without smoking. If you want to start exercising regularly, your goal might be to exercise for 30 minutes thrice a week.

- **Make a plan for changing your habits.** Once you have set specific goals, develop a plan for changing your habits. This plan should include steps that you will take to achieve your goals. For example, if your goal is to quit smoking, your plan might include avoiding triggers, finding healthy coping mechanisms, and seeking support from others.

- **Take small steps.** It is important to take small steps when you are trying to change your habits. If you try to change too many habits at once, you will likely get overwhelmed and give up. Start by focusing on changing one habit at a time.

- **Be patient and persistent.** It takes time to develop new habits. Don't get discouraged if you don't see results immediately. Just keep practicing your new habits; eventually, they will become second nature.

Chapter 7: The Warrior's Code of Ethics

Warriors live by a code of ethics. This code of ethics guides their behavior and helps them make decisions aligned with their values. The five core values of the warrior code of ethics are integrity, honor, respect, courage, and compassion.

Integrity

Integrity is the quality of being honest and having strong moral principles. It is a virtue essential for living a good and meaningful life. Warriors are often seen as paragons of integrity because they are trained to be honest, courageous, and principled.

Integrity is more than just being honest. It is also about having a strong moral compass and always striving to do what is right, even when difficult. People with integrity are trustworthy, reliable, and fair. They are also courageous enough to stand up for what they believe in, even when it is unpopular.

Integrity is important for several reasons. First, it allows us to build strong relationships with others. When people know they can trust us to be honest and fair, they are more likely to open up and share their deepest thoughts and feelings, leading to deeper and more meaningful relationships.

Second, integrity is essential for success in all areas of life. Employers look for honest, reliable, and strong work ethic employees. Teachers look for students who are willing to put in the effort and who are honest about their work. Friends look for people they can count on and who are always there for them.

Third, integrity is simply the right thing to do. Living our lives with integrity means we are true to ourselves and our values. We are also setting a good example for others.

Be honest with yourself. The first step to developing integrity is being honest about your values and beliefs. What is important to you? What do you stand for? Once you know what you believe in, making decisions consistent with those beliefs becomes easier.

Do the right thing, even when it's difficult. It's easy to be honest and principled when things are going well. However, the true test of integrity comes when faced with difficult choices. When we are tempted to take the easy way out or do something we know is wrong, it is important to remember our values and stand up for what is right.

Be accountable. When we make mistakes, we must be accountable for our actions. This means taking responsibility for our mistakes and apologizing to those affected by them. It also means learning from our mistakes and trying to do better in the future.

Honor

Honor is a quality often associated with warriors, but it is something anyone can strive for. Honor is about living your life in accordance with your values and beliefs, being honest and fair in your dealings with others, and being courageous enough to stand up for what you believe in.

One of the most important things you can do to develop honor is to live your life in accordance with your values and beliefs. What is important to you? What do you believe in? Once you know your values and beliefs, you can start living your life in a way that reflects them.

This means being honest and fair in your dealings with others. It means keeping your promises and honoring your commitments. It means standing up for what you believe in, even when it is difficult.

Being honorable also means being courageous. It means having the courage to do what is right, even when it is unpopular. It means having the courage to stand up for what you believe in, even when you are outnumbered.

Imagine that you are working on a group project for school. One of your team members is not pulling their weight. They are not showing up to meetings and not completing their assigned tasks. You could easily relax and let your team members' lack of effort go unnoticed, but this would not be honorable.

Instead, you decide to talk to your team member about the situation. You explain to them that their lack of effort is unfair to the rest of the team and puts the project at risk. Your team member is initially reluctant to change their behavior, but you are persistent. You continue to talk to them about the situation and offer to help them with their work.

Eventually, your team members start to contribute. They start attending meetings and completing their assigned tasks. The project is completed on time, and the team receives a good grade. By standing up to your team members and encouraging them to contribute, you demonstrated honor. You put the team's needs ahead of your own, and you helped ensure that everyone was working together for a common goal.

Developing honor is important because it helps you to build trust and respect with others. It also helps you to live a more fulfilling and meaningful life. When you live your life in accordance with your values and beliefs, you are more likely to be happy and successful.

Respect

Respect is the foundation of strong relationships. It is the glue that holds us together and allows us to build trust and rapport with others. When we respect someone, we show them that we value their feelings, opinions, and rights. We treat them with dignity and kindness, even when we disagree with them.

Respect is especially important in the world of warriors. Warriors know everyone deserves to be treated with respect, regardless of rank, status, or beliefs. They also know respecting their enemies is essential for building trust and understanding.

Here are some tips for developing respect for yourself and others:

1. Respect yourself. The first step to developing respect for others is to respect yourself. This means being kind and compassionate to yourself, accepting yourself for who you are, and setting boundaries. When you respect yourself, you are more likely to demand the same respect from others.

2. Be mindful of your words and actions. When you communicate with others, be mindful of your words and actions. Avoid using hurtful or disrespectful language, and respect their opinions and beliefs, even if you disagree with them.

3. Listen to others. Listening is a skill we all take for granted, but it is one of the most important skills we can learn. When we listen effectively, we can build stronger relationships, learn new things, and resolve conflict more peacefully. Active listening is more than just hearing what someone is saying. It is about paying attention to their words, body language, and tone of voice and responding in a way that shows that you understand.

Active listening is a skill that can be learned and improved with practice. Active listening is important for several reasons.

- First, it shows the speaker that you respect them and their thoughts. When you give someone your full attention, it tells them that you are interested in what they have to say. This can help build trust and rapport.

- Second, active listening helps you to learn more effectively. You are more likely to remember what the speaker is saying when actively listening. You are also more likely to understand complex concepts.

- Third, active listening can help you to resolve conflict more peacefully. When you actively listen to someone who is upset, you are more likely to understand their perspective and find a solution that works for everyone involved.

4. Be honest and trustworthy. Honesty and trustworthiness are two of the most important qualities that a person can have. They are essential for building respect in all areas of life, from personal relationships to professional settings. When you are honest and trustworthy, others know they can rely on you. They know that you will keep your word, that you will be upfront with them, and that you will always act in their best interests.

Respect is essential for building strong and healthy relationships. It shows that you value the other person, listen to them, and consider their thoughts and feelings. Respect also creates a sense of safety and security in relationships. Knowing that the other person respects you makes you feel more comfortable being yourself and sharing your thoughts and feelings.

Honesty and trustworthiness build respect by showing others that you are dependable. When you are honest, you show that you value the truth and are willing to be accountable for your actions. When you are trustworthy, you show that you can be relied upon to keep your promises and to act in the best interests of others.

Be fair and just. We live in a diverse world where people come from all walks of life. We may have different backgrounds, beliefs, and values, but one thing that should unite us all is our shared humanity. We all deserve to be treated with fairness and justice, regardless of our differences.

Treating someone fairly means giving them the same opportunities and respect as you would anyone else. It means being impartial and unbiased in your dealings with them. It also means being open-minded and willing to learn about their perspective, even if you disagree with it.

Justice is about upholding the rule of law and ensuring that everyone is treated equally under the law. It's about protecting the rights of all people, regardless of their background or beliefs. It's also about holding people accountable for their actions and ensuring justice.

Be willing to forgive. Everyone makes mistakes. When someone you respect makes a mistake, be willing to forgive them. Forgiveness doesn't mean that you condone their behavior, but it does mean that you are willing to move on and maintain a relationship with them.

Courage

Courage is the ability to face danger or difficulty without fear. Warriors are always courageous. They do not let fear hold them back from achieving their goals.

But courage is not just for warriors. Courage is for everyone. It is the quality that allows us to stand up for what we believe in, even when it is difficult. It is the quality that allows us to take risks, even when we are afraid.

Rosa Parks was an African American woman who refused to give up her seat on a bus to a white man in 1955. Her courage sparked the Montgomery Bus Boycott, which helped end segregation on buses in the United States.

Nelson Mandela was a South African anti-apartheid revolutionary, political leader, and philanthropist who served as President of South Africa from 1994 to 1999. He was the country's first black head of state and the first elected in a fully representative democratic election. His government focused on dismantling the legacy of apartheid by tackling institutionalized racism and fostering racial reconciliation. I admire him for his courage in standing up against apartheid, even though he was imprisoned for 27 years for his activism.

Malala Yousafzai is a Pakistani activist for female education and the youngest Nobel Prize laureate. When she was just 15 years old, she was shot by the Taliban for speaking out about her right to an education. She survived the attack and continued to advocate for girls' education worldwide.

One way to develop courage is to face your fears. Step outside of your comfort zone and do things that make you uncomfortable. The more you face your fears, the more courageous you will become.

Another way to develop courage is to practice standing up for what you believe in. Start small by standing up to bullies or by speaking out against injustice. As you become more comfortable standing up for your beliefs, you will find you are more courageous in other areas of your life.

Finally, you can develop courage by taking risks. Step outside of your comfort zone and try new things. Even if you fail, you will learn from your experience and become more courageous as a result. Here are some specific examples of how to develop courage in different areas of your life:

- **At work:** Speak up in meetings, even if you have unpopular ideas. Volunteer for new projects, even if they are challenging. Stand up for your colleagues, even if it means confronting your boss.

- **In your relationships:** Be honest with your loved ones, even when it is difficult. Speak up for yourself, even if it means setting boundaries. Stand up for your loved ones, even if it means confronting someone who is hurting them.

- **In your community:** Get involved in causes that you care about. Speak out against injustice, even if it means facing opposition. Stand up for the rights of others, even if they are different from you.

Compassion

Imagine a world where everyone is compassionate. A world where everyone understands and cares about the suffering of others. A world where everyone is willing to help those in need. This is the world that warriors strive to create.

Compassion is a key quality of any warrior. It allows us to see the humanity in our enemies and to treat them with dignity, even in the midst of conflict. It motivates us to fight for justice and to protect the innocent. But compassion is not something that we are born with. It is a skill that must be developed and practiced. Here are a few tips for developing compassion as a warrior:

1. Put yourself in other people's shoes. One of the best ways to develop compassion is to see things from other people's perspectives. When you see someone suffering, imagine what it would be like to be in their place. What would you be feeling? What would you need? This exercise can help you to develop empathy, which is the ability to understand and share the feelings of others. Empathy is essential for compassion.

Here is a simple exercise to practice empathy: Choose someone you know, such as a friend, family member, or colleague. Think about a time when they were suffering. What were they going through? How did they feel?

Close your eyes and try to imagine yourself in their shoes. What would it be like to experience what they experienced? Once you have a good understanding of their perspective, open your eyes and ask yourself: "What would I need if I was in their situation?"

2. Be willing to help others in need. Another way to develop compassion is to be willing to help others in need. This doesn't mean you must solve all of the world's problems. But even small acts of kindness can make a big difference in someone's life.

3. Practice self-compassion. It's important to remember that compassion is not just about helping others. It's also about being compassionate towards yourself. This means understanding and accepting yourself, even when you make mistakes. When you are kind to yourself, you are more likely to be kind to others. So make sure to take care of yourself and to be gentle with yourself.

Here are a few tips for practicing self-compassion:

- Be kind and understanding towards yourself when you make mistakes.

- Accept yourself for who you are, flaws and all.

- Take care of your physical and mental health.

- Practice self-affirmation by saying positive things to yourself.

4. Study the lives of compassionate warriors. There are many great examples of compassionate warriors throughout history. People like Nelson Mandela, Mother Teresa, and Mahatma Gandhi were known for their compassion and commitment to helping others. Studying the lives of these compassionate warriors can inspire us to be more compassionate. It can also teach us valuable lessons about how to develop compassion and how to use it to make a difference in the world.

Chapter 8: The Warrior's Way in Business

B usiness is a battlefield, and the warrior mindset can help entre-preneurs and leaders succeed. In business, the warrior's way is more than just a strategy; it's a way of thinking that turns challenges into victories and setbacks into chances to learn. As you learn more about the warrior's way in business, remember that it's not just about making money and taking over the market; it's about building a legacy of fearlessness, innovation, and ethical leadership. In this chapter, we'll learn more about the warrior's path, including the mental strength, emotional resilience, and unyielding courage that make a fearless warrior.

Applying the Warrior Mindset to Business

Like in warfare, strategic thinking is paramount to your success. Embrace this mindset, recognizing that risks are mere stepping stones to greatness and challenges are opportunities waiting to be seized. See every setback as a valuable lesson, not a failure.

To truly embody the warrior spirit in business, start by setting crystal-clear goals and objectives. Warriors have a keen sense of what they want to achieve. They don't just dream; they meticulously plan their path to victory. Envision your goals, visualize your triumphs, and lay down a meticulously crafted roadmap toward your objectives.

Discipline and focus are your trusted allies. Like a warrior honing his skills, stay disciplined and maintain unwavering focus. Discipline is the key to unlocking your full potential. It is the ability to control your impulses, stay focused on your goals, and consistently work towards them, even in adversity. Focus is the laser beam that guides your discipline, ensuring you remain on the path to success.

Distractions are like fleeting shadows, ever-present but ultimately meaningless. They may lure you off track, but you must resist their temptation. Your concentration is your weapon against them. When you are focused, you are unstoppable.

Be relentless in your pursuit of your goals. Channel all your energy towards your objectives and never give up, no matter how difficult the journey may seem. The warrior mindset demands dedication, and through discipline, you harness the power to overcome any obstacle.

Imagine you are a student who wants to get good grades in your classes. You know that you need to study hard, but you also have many other commitments, such as extracurricular activities and social events.

To achieve your goal, you need to be disciplined and focused. You need to create a study schedule and stick to it, even if it means turning down social invitations. You also need to eliminate distractions when you are studying. This means turning off your phone, closing your email, and finding a quiet place to work.

If you struggle to stay focused, break down your study sessions into smaller chunks. For example, you could set a timer for 25 minutes and focus on studying one topic during that time. Once the timer goes off, take a short break and start again. It is also important to reward yourself for your progress. For example, if you complete a study

session, you could allow yourself to watch a TV show or play a video
game for a short time.

Embrace risk-taking with open arms. Warriors understand that the
path to success is paved with risks. Fortune favors the bold, and warriors are willing to tread where others fear. Do not shy away from challenges; confront them head-on. It's in these daring moves that your
true potential unfolds. Each risk you take is a leap toward unparalleled
growth and achievement.

When adversity knocks on your door, welcome it as a fellow warrior. Perseverance is your battle cry. Warriors do not crumble in adversity; they rise, stronger and more determined. Each setback is a test of
your resilience. See it as an opportunity to showcase your unwavering
spirit. Embrace the challenges, learn from them, and let them fortify
your resolve.

Stay agile in your strategies. Warriors adapt swiftly to changing circumstances. The business world is just as volatile and unpredictable as a battlefield. New technologies emerge overnight, customer preferences shift constantly, and the competition is always looking for ways to gain an edge. In this environment, businesses that cannot adapt quickly are doomed to fail.

Agility is the key to survival and success in the modern business world. It means being open to new ideas, embracing change, and evolving with the market. It means being able to identify and respond to opportunities and threats quickly. It means pivoting your strategies when necessary without sacrificing your long-term goals.

Netflix is a classic example of a company that has stayed agile and successful in a rapidly changing industry. The company started as a DVD-by-mail service, but it quickly pivoted to streaming video when it became clear that this was the future of the industry. Netflix has also quickly embraced new technologies like smart TVs and mobile devices.

Netflix's success is due in large part to its agile culture. The company encourages employees to experiment and take risks. It also has a rapid feedback loop, allowing the company to learn from its mistakes and adjust its strategies quickly. For example, when Netflix first launched its streaming service, it was only available on a small number of devices. However, the company quickly expanded the availability of its service to meet customer demand.

Netflix's commitment to agility has helped it stay ahead of the competition and become one of the world's most successful companies.

Maintain a laser-like focus on your goals amidst the chaos of the market. Let the noise of the business world fade into the background as you concentrate on your objectives. The warrior mindset demands clarity and determination. Ask yourself, with every decision you make, if this aligns with your goals. If the answer is yes, proceed with the confidence of a warrior stepping onto the battlefield. Your unwavering focus will guide you, ensuring you emerge victorious in the ever-changing business landscape.

Developing a Warrior Culture

A warrior culture is a business culture that fosters an environment of fearlessness, ambition, and shared purpose. It is built on trust, mutual respect, and a collective commitment to excellence. In a warrior culture, employees are encouraged to voice their ideas and concerns without fear of reprisal. Risk-taking is celebrated, mistakes are seen as opportunities for growth, and every challenge is viewed as a chance to prove the team's resilience.

A warrior culture can help businesses to achieve their goals in several ways. First, it can help to attract and retain top talent. People want to work for leaders and organizations that believe in them and empower them to do their best work. Second, a warrior culture can help to drive innovation and creativity. When employees feel comfortable taking risks and sharing their ideas, new products, services, and processes are more likely to be developed. Third, a warrior culture can help to create a more cohesive and productive workplace. When employees feel supported and respected by their colleagues, they are more likely to be engaged in their work and committed to the team's success.

You can do many things to develop a warrior culture in your business. Here are a few tips:

- **Set clear expectations and goals.** Everyone in your organization should know what is expected of them and what the team is working towards. Communicate your vision and values clearly and regularly.

- **Celebrate success.** When your team achieves a goal, celebrate it! This will help motivate them and keep them focused on their goals.

- **Learn from failures.** Failure is a part of life. Don't beat yourself up about it. Instead, learn from your mistakes and move on.

- **Create a supportive environment.** Warriors support each other. They help each other to learn and grow. Create a supportive environment where people feel comfortable taking risks and asking for help.

- **Empower your employees.** Give them the authority to make decisions and take action. This will help them feel more invested in their work and more responsible for the team's success.

Here are a few key elements of a warrior culture:

1. Fearlessness: Warriors are not afraid to take risks. They know that failure is a part of the learning process and are willing to step outside their comfort zone to achieve their goals.

2. Ambition: Warriors are driven to succeed. They have a clear vision for what they want to achieve and are relentlessly pursuing their goals.

3. Shared purpose: Warriors are united by a shared purpose. They know what they are fighting for and are committed to working together to achieve it.

4. Trust and respect: Warriors trust and respect each other. They know that they can rely on their team members to have their backs, no matter what.

5. Commitment to excellence: Warriors are committed to excellence in everything they do. They strive to be the best at what they do and never settle for anything less.

Leadership in the Warrior's Way

In the realm of leadership, there stands a warrior class. These leaders are not defined by their authoritative control but by their unwavering strength, compassion, and unwavering commitment to guiding others toward greatness.

A fundamental aspect of warrior leadership lies in leading by example. These leaders do not just talk the talk; they walk the walk. Their actions echo their words, displaying the values they uphold. This consistency builds trust and respect among team members, fostering a collaborative environment where everyone feels valued and understood.

Imagine a warrior leader who preaches the importance of hard work and dedication. However, they are often seen leaving the office early or taking long breaks. This hypocrisy will not go unnoticed by the team. Their actions will speak louder than words, undermining their credibility and authority.

In contrast, a warrior leader who embodies their values through their actions inspires and motivates others. They are willing to roll up their sleeves and work alongside their team, demonstrating their commitment to the shared cause. This authenticity earns the respect and admiration of team members, creating a foundation for trust and collaboration.

Another hallmark of warrior leadership is clarity in direction. These leaders provide a clear roadmap, outlining the path to success. Ambitious yet achievable goals are set, challenging the team to push their boundaries while ensuring the objectives are within reach. This balance prevents overwhelming pressure and instills a sense of purpose and determination.

Imagine a team without a clear vision or goals. They would be like a ship without a rudder, adrift at sea. Uncertainty and confusion would breed frustration and resentment, hindering productivity and success.

A warrior leader provides the team with clear direction, painting a vivid picture of the desired outcome. They break down ambitious goals into smaller, more manageable steps, making the journey seem less daunting. By providing clarity and purpose, warrior leaders empower their teams to achieve their full potential.

Warrior leaders understand the power of camaraderie. They cultivate a sense of belonging within the team, emphasizing that everyone plays a crucial role in the collective journey. Acknowledging and celebrating the team's efforts and accomplishments become second nature to these leaders. Such recognition fuels motivation and instills a deep sense of pride and dedication. Team members feel seen and appreciated, fostering loyalty and a strong sense of commitment.

Imagine a team where individual contributions are overlooked and team success is not celebrated. Such an environment would be devoid of motivation and inspiration. Team members would feel undervalued and unappreciated, leading to high turnover rates and low morale.

A warrior leader fosters camaraderie by creating a supportive and inclusive environment. They recognize and celebrate the team's achievements, both big and small. This recognition validates the team's hard work and dedication, strengthening their bond and commitment to the shared cause.

Warrior leaders possess the ability to recognize and leverage each team member's unique strengths. They understand that diversity in skills and perspectives enhances the team's capabilities. By tapping into these individual strengths, leaders create a synergy that propels the organization toward its objectives.

Imagine a team where everyone is expected to perform the same tasks, regardless of their skills and interests. This approach would stifle creativity and innovation, hindering the team's potential.

A warrior leader recognizes the value of individual strengths. They create a tailored approach, assigning tasks and responsibilities that align with each team member's unique skills and interests. This allows team members to play to their strengths, contributing to the team's success in a meaningful way. Additionally, it fosters a sense of fulfillment and engagement, motivating team members to perform their best.

Compassion is a cornerstone of warrior leadership. These leaders empathize with their team members, understanding their struggles and challenges. Compassionate leadership does not equate to leniency; it means offering support and guidance while maintaining accountability. Warrior leaders inspire through kindness and understanding, creating a supportive atmosphere where team members are encouraged to learn from failures and grow stronger.

Imagine a team leader who is quick to criticize and blame but reluctant to offer praise or support. Such a leader would create a toxic work environment, breeding fear and resentment.

A warrior leader leads with compassion. They understand that everyone makes mistakes. When team members fall short, they offer constructive feedback and guidance, helping them to learn from their mistakes.

Building a Warrior Team

A warrior team is a group of high-performing individuals committed to achieving their goals. They are disciplined, focused, and resilient. They are also supportive and collaborative and celebrate each other's successes. If you want to build a warrior team, here are a few things you can do:

1. Hire the right people. The foundation of any great team is made up of great individuals. When hiring new team members, look for people who align with your values and have the skills and experience necessary to succeed. But don't just focus on technical skills. Look for people who are also motivated, passionate, and have a strong work ethic.

Here are a few tips for hiring the right people:

- Be clear about your values and expectations. What qualities are important to you as a team member? Once you know what you're looking for, you can screen candidates based on those qualities.

- Ask the right questions during interviews. Instead of asking generic questions about someone's experience, ask more specific questions about how they've handled challenges and achieved success in the past.

- Get feedback from others. Once you've narrowed down your candidates, ask other people for their feedback on them. This could include former colleagues, managers, or even friends and family.

2. Provide training and development. Once you've hired the right people, it's important to invest in their training and development. This will help them grow their skills and knowledge and show them that you're committed to their success. Here are a few ways to provide training and development for your team members:

- Offer formal training programs. This could include in-house training programs, online courses, or conferences.

- Encourage team members to attend industry events. This is a great way for them to learn about their field's latest trends and developments.

- Provide opportunities for on-the-job training. This could involve shadowing more experienced team members, working on new projects, or taking on new challenges.

3. Create a culture of collaboration. Collaboration is essential for any team that wants to succeed. When team members collaborate effectively, they can learn from each other, share ideas, and solve problems more effectively. Here are a few ways to create a culture of collaboration on your team:

- Encourage team members to communicate openly and honestly with each other. This means creating a safe space where team members feel comfortable sharing their ideas and feedback, even if it's different from what others are saying.

- Provide opportunities for team members to work together on projects. This could involve cross-functional teams, team-building activities, or informal brainstorming sessions.

- Recognize and reward team members for collaborating effectively. This could involve public recognition, financial rewards, or a simple thank you.

4. Celebrate success. When your team achieves a goal, it's important to celebrate their success. This shows them that you appreciate their hard work and dedication and motivates them to keep up the good work. Here are a few ways to celebrate success with your team:

- Throw a team party or lunch. This is a great way to get everyone together and celebrate their accomplishments.

- Give public recognition to team members who have gone above and beyond. This could be done in a team meeting, company newsletter, or social media.

- Offer financial rewards for team success. This could involve bonuses, commissions, or other forms of financial compensation.

Building a warrior team takes time and effort, but it's worth it. Warrior teams are more productive, innovative, and likely to achieve their goals. By following the tips above, you can start building a warrior team of your own.

Chapter 9: Using Warrior Wisdom in Today's World of Business and Life

H ave you ever wondered why many business people carry copies of The Art of War by Sun Tzu? At first, I thought it was just a trendy thing to do, like a fashion statement. But then I began to see the real value in those ancient warrior principles.

I realized that beneath the surface, the advice from these old texts is incredibly valuable, even in today's high-tech age. While they won't teach you how to use software programs like MS Word, they offer great insights into marketing, leadership, and managing resources.

For example, Sun Tzu talks a lot about strategy and being adaptable. In today's fast-paced digital world, where things change all the time, being able to plan ahead and adjust to new situations is super important. His ideas about leadership still hold true today—things like motivating your team and keeping everyone working together towards a common goal.

What's cool is that these principles can be applied to all sorts of situations. Whether it's solving problems at work or coming up with new ideas for a project, the wisdom from these ancient texts can really help. So, even though these ideas were first used in battles with swords and arrows, they're still relevant today. By learning from the past, we can better handle the challenges of the present and set ourselves up for future success.

With that perspective in mind, let's delve into some of the most impactful quotes and lessons from these ancient texts, ones you can easily integrate into your daily office routine to foster loyalty and productivity. And just to spice things up, we'll sprinkle in a bit of Machiavelli's wisdom from "The Prince," originally crafted as a guide for Italian royalty but surprisingly relevant to modern leadership.

It's intriguing, isn't it? These texts, initially aimed at historical war-riors and rulers, now hold a revered place among business profes-sionals, relationship experts, and beyond. It speaks volumes about the enduring relevance of the warrior mindset, which you'll soon discover echoes much of what we've already discussed.

Let's start with insights from "The Art of War"

The idea that nations don't benefit from long wars teaches us that prolonged conflicts are pointless. If you disagree with someone, getting into a long fight will tire you both out and cause damage. It's like winning a battle but losing so much that it's not a victory. Instead of fighting, turn your opponents into friends and find solutions that help everyone.

Remember, a real warrior doesn't jump into every fight. Choosing your battles wisely shows strength. It's not about being aggressive or reacting quickly; it's about staying calm, forgiving, and using your power wisely.

Sun Tzu, a famous military strategist, said, "the best victory is when you win without fighting." This is even more relevant today, where smart strategies often lead to bigger wins than direct battles.

Think about the saying, "Opportunities multiply as they are seized." It means taking action brings rewards. Just like Arnold Schwarzenegger used bodybuilding to become successful, we can make smart choices to turn small starts into big accomplishments.

Sun Tzu also said it's important to "know the enemy and know yourself." This is crucial in business and life. Understanding your strengths and weaknesses, as well as those of your competitors, is key to success. Ignoring these things can lead to disaster.

Outside of work, knowing yourself helps you set goals and values. Sun Tzu's idea of a great leader who cares more about their duty than personal glory matches Seneca's philosophy of simplicity and goodness. In the workplace, it's important to be humble and focus on serving others instead of your ego. Being a leader who cares more about the team's success than their fame leads to success for everyone.

Now, let's draw from Machiavelli's timeless counsel:

In "The Prince," Machiavelli shares tips for good leadership, but his ideas go beyond just politics. They give us useful tips on how to lead effectively. One important lesson is about looking virtuous while also being practical in what you do. In today's workplace, this means showing honesty while making smart decisions that help everyone. It's about balancing doing what's right and dealing with real-life situations—a skill crucial for modern leaders.

Machiavelli also talks about the importance of being flexible and thinking ahead. Leaders need to expect problems and change their plans when needed, just like a smart general does in a battle. Being flexible and thinking ahead helps leaders handle tough situations confidently, staying ahead of the competition.

If you want to keep succeeding, adjusting how you do things according to the times is crucial. This is super important, especially if you're leading a big company and might start feeling too comfortable. Always stay one step ahead to avoid ending up like Kodak.

Remember, it's okay to change your principles if needed, but it should come from you, not others.

Treat people well or deal with them decisively. Small issues can lead to retaliation, while big ones can make it impossible to make things right. While it's not cool to crush your opponents or team members (fun fact: Sun Tsu is more about making peace than Machiavelli), the idea is still solid: don't make enemies and let them recover.

It's best for everyone if you avoid fights and try to make everyone happy. But if you have to compete, be quick about it. Smart people act fast, while fools drag their feet, and wasting time is like throwing away money.

Entrepreneurs are good at seeing obstacles and opportunities as pretty much the same thing, and they know how to make the most of both. Even something simple, like opening a can of beans, can be seen as a challenge or an opportunity. As we talked about before, facing challenges can help you grow. It's pretty cool how Machiavelli's advice still works for entrepreneurs today.

This just goes to show that the warrior mindset is timeless and still important today. With a warrior's attitude, you can approach anything. I really recommend checking out these books to help you grow and become the best version of yourself. They're must-reads for anyone wanting to embrace their inner warrior.

Chapter 10: The Warrior's Journey

The warrior's journey is not easy. It is a long and difficult trip but also a journey of change and growth. It is a journey to the depths of your mind and the world's challenges.

Every challenge, ally, and victory on the warrior's journey is like a thread in a tapestry, creating a story of change and victory. As you go on your warrior's journey, remember that it is not just about reaching the end but learning and growing along the way. In this chapter, we will explore the warrior's journey, similar to the hero's journey. We will learn about the challenges and triumphs, the obstacles and allies, and the victory that awaits those brave enough to walk the path of fearlessness.

Overcoming Obstacles

In your warrior's journey, challenges are not roadblocks but stepping stones. Every obstacle you encounter is a chance to test your mettle, to push your limits, and to emerge stronger. Instead of being deterred, you face challenges head-on, acknowledging them as opportunities to refine your skills and character. Your warrior spirit fuels your determination to conquer these hurdles, knowing that each triumph over adversity is a testament to your resilience.

Fear is a natural part of any journey, but warriors do not let it control them. You confront your fears with courage, understanding that growth often lies just beyond your comfort zone. Taking risks becomes second nature, for you comprehend that great accomplishments seldom arise from the safety of familiarity. Each risk becomes a stepping stone, leading you closer to your goals. Your bravery becomes a beacon, inspiring others to face their fears and challenges with similar fortitude.

Mistakes are not signs of weakness but growth opportunities. As a warrior, you embrace your mistakes, extracting valuable lessons from each experience. Instead of dwelling on failures, you analyze them objectively, understanding the root causes and determining how to avoid similar pitfalls in the future. Every setback becomes a chance to refine your strategies, making you more adept and prepared for future challenges. Your ability to learn from mistakes sets you apart, ensuring that you continually evolve and adapt on your journey.

Adversity is a constant companion on the warrior's path. However, you do not succumb to despair or give in to hardships. Your unwavering perseverance becomes your greatest weapon. No matter how daunting the challenges, you persist with unyielding determination. You draw strength from within, tapping into your resilience to navigate through the toughest times. Your ability to endure inspires those around you, reminding them of the power of sheer determination in the face of adversity.

In the face of challenges, visualization becomes your guiding light. You close your eyes and vividly imagine yourself overcoming obstacles, achieving your goals, and embracing success. Visualization is not merely a mental exercise but a powerful tool that programs your mind for triumph. You visualize the result and the steps you need to take to get there. This mental imagery becomes a roadmap, guiding your actions and decisions. With each visualization session, you reinforce your belief in your abilities, amplifying your confidence and motivation.

Every small victory matters on your warrior's journey. You celebrate the grand triumphs and the minor achievements along the way. No matter how insignificant, each milestone reached is a testament to your progress. Your celebrations are not just moments of joy but also opportunities for reflection. You acknowledge the hard work, dedication, and perseverance that led to each victory, fueling your motivation for the challenges. These celebrations fuel your spirit, propelling you forward with renewed vigor and determination.

Your warrior's journey is a testament to your courage, resilience, and determination. Embracing challenges, facing fears, learning from mistakes, persevering in adversity, harnessing the power of visualization, and celebrating every victory are the cornerstones of your path. With each step, you grow stronger, wiser, and more capable. Your journey is not just a pursuit of goals but a transformative odyssey that shapes you into the best version of yourself. Keep forging ahead, for

every challenge overcome brings you closer to the ultimate victory –
the victory of becoming the warrior you were destined to be.

Finding Your Allies

As a warrior, you know the path ahead will be fraught with obstacles,
but you are determined to persevere. Your journey is not a solitary one,
however. You have a band of trusted allies by your side, each offering
their unique strengths and support.

Your allies are more than just companions. They are pillars of
strength, sources of wisdom, and shields against adversity. They come
from all walks of life, united by their belief in you and their commitment to seeing you succeed. In their presence, you feel empowered,
supported, and inspired.

True allies see you beyond your limitations. They recognize the greatness within you and encourage you to reach your full potential. They understand the depths of your soul and the dreams that burn in your heart. When you stumble, they help you rise again. When you falter, they whisper words of encouragement. And when you triumph, they celebrate your victory with joyful abandon.

Your allies are not merely passive observers on the sidelines. They are active participants in your journey. They cheer you on, challenge you to grow, and offer their guidance when needed. They are your sounding board, your confidants, and your trusted advisors. With their support, you can overcome any obstacle and achieve any goal.

Your allies are out there, waiting to be found. Be open to connections, both within your existing circle and beyond. Seek out those whose values align with yours and whose energy resonates with your soul. Build relationships based on mutual respect, trust, and understanding.

Remember, alliances are not one-sided. As you receive support from your allies, be prepared to offer the same in return. Listen to their stories, empathize with their struggles, and celebrate their victories. Be the shoulder they can lean on and the hand that helps them most when needed. Through reciprocity, the bond between warriors and their allies grows stronger, creating a force to be reckoned with.

Your allies play a vital role in cultivating resilience within you. They remind you of your strengths when doubt creeps in and offer hope when the path ahead seems shrouded in darkness. With their support, you can bounce back from setbacks and emerge even stronger than before.

Your allies also help you to see the world through a new lens. They share their unique perspectives and experiences, broadening your horizons and deepening your understanding of life. In their presence, you learn to grow and evolve as a warrior.

Your allies come from all walks of life, each with their own unique gifts and talents. Embrace their diversity; it will enrich your journey and make you a stronger warrior. From their wisdom and experience, you can learn and grow. Together, you form a tapestry of strength, resilience, and compassion.

Achieving Your Victory

As a warrior on a journey, you embrace challenges as opportunities to grow and evolve. You cultivate resilience, your armor against setbacks. You harness the power of visualization to guide you toward your goals. You nurture self-compassion, your constant companion through trials and triumphs. And you build a supportive network of like-minded individuals to cheer you on.

Challenges are an inevitable part of the warrior's journey. They test your strength, courage, and resolve. But they also offer valuable lessons, helping you to discover your inner potential and resilience. When faced with a challenge, don't shrink back in fear. Instead, meet it head-on with determination and unwavering belief in yourself.

Resilience is the ability to bounce back from setbacks stronger than before. It is your armor against the inevitable challenges of life. To cultivate resilience, develop a steadfast mindset that enables you to persevere, even when the path seems daunting. View setbacks as temporary learning opportunities, and embrace them as part of your journey.

Visualization is a powerful tool for manifesting your desires and achieving your goals. Visualize your success vividly in your mind. See yourself conquering challenges, achieving milestones, and celebrating your victories. Visualization fuels your determination and conviction, clearing the path to your goals. It also instills confidence, helping you face uncertainties with unwavering belief in your abilities.

Self-compassion is your constant companion on the warrior's journey. It is the kindness and understanding you offer yourself, even when you make mistakes or fall short. Treat yourself with the same compassion you would extend to a friend. Embrace your mistakes as opportunities to learn and grow. A positive inner dialogue will encourage you during difficult times and help you to persevere.

On your warrior's journey, you don't travel alone. Surround yourself with a supportive network of like-minded individuals who understand your aspirations and challenges. These connections provide
a safety net, offering encouragement when you falter and celebrating
your big and small victories. Share your dreams with these individuals;
their belief in your potential is a powerful catalyst, propelling you
forward.

As you reach the pinnacle of your journey, you realize that victory
is not merely an external triumph. It is the culmination of your inner
transformation, a testament to your unwavering spirit and dedication.
Your victory is a beacon of inspiration for others, showcasing the
remarkable power of resilience, visualization, and self-compassion. It
echoes the truth that every challenge, every setback, and every moment
of doubt was worth it.

Your victory reminds us that within us lies the strength to overcome any obstacle and the capacity to emerge from challenges not just unscathed but triumphant.

Chapter II: The Warrior's Legacy

The warrior mindset is a way of life that involves overcoming your fears and challenges, positively impacting the world, and inspiring others to do the same. When you embrace this mindset, you accept the responsibility to be courageous, compassionate, and strong. This chapter will explore what it means to leave a warrior's legacy.

As you journey through life as a warrior, remember that your legacy will not happen in the distant future; it is being created right now with every choice you make and every action you take. Consider the impact you can have on the world, the people you can help, and the inspiration you can provide. Your legacy is not a destination but an ongoing story of your fearlessness, shaping the world and inspiring future generations.

Leaving a Positive Impact on the World

Warriors are often associated with fighting and winning battles, but they are about more than that. They are also about using their skills and talents to impact the world positively.

As a warrior, you have the power to leave a lasting legacy. You can inspire others, make a difference in the lives of those around you, and create a better world for future generations. Here are a few ways that you can leave a positive impact on the world as a warrior:

1. Be a beacon of hope and inspiration. As a warrior, you are a force to be reckoned with. You have faced challenges and overcome obstacles, and you continue to fight for what you believe in. You are an inspiration to others, and you have the power to make a difference in the world.

One of the most powerful things you can do as a warrior is to be a beacon of hope and inspiration to others. Show the world that overcoming obstacles, achieving your dreams, and making a difference is possible.

- Share your story. One of the best ways to inspire others is to share your story. Talk about the challenges you have faced and how you overcame them. Share your victories and setbacks, and let people know it's okay to fail as long as they pick themselves up and keep going. Your story can be a source of hope and inspiration for others facing their challenges.

- Be an example of resilience, perseverance, and strength. When others see you facing challenges and setbacks with courage and resilience, it inspires them to do the same. Show them that it is possible to overcome anything, no matter how difficult.

- Be supportive and encouraging. Offer your support and encouragement to others who are struggling. Let them know that you believe in them and are there for them. Your support can make a big difference in their lives.

2. Use your skills and talents to help others. Every warrior has unique skills and talents that they can use to make a difference in the world. As a warrior, you are strong, courageous, and compassionate. You are also resourceful and resilient. You have overcome challenges and obstacles in your life, and you have emerged stronger and wiser.

It is time to use your skills and talents to help others. Think about what you are good at and what you enjoy doing. What are your passions and interests? What are your strengths and weaknesses? Once you understand yourself well, you can start thinking about using your gifts to make a difference in the world.

- Teach and mentor. If you have a knack for teaching, you can volunteer your time to tutor children or mentor youth. Many organizations need volunteers to help students with schoolwork, provide career guidance, or offer support and encouragement.

- Protect the environment. If you are passionate about environmental protection, you can join a local environmental organization. You can volunteer to clean up parks and waterways, plant trees, or advocate for sustainable policies.

- Use your creative talents. If you have a gift for music, art, or writing, you can use your talents to bring joy and inspiration to others. You can volunteer your time to perform at nursing homes or hospitals, teach art classes to children, or write stories for children's magazines.

3. Stand up for what you believe in. Warriors for justice and equality are not afraid to stand up for what they believe in, even when it's unpopular. They are not afraid to speak out against injustice and oppression. They use their voices to advocate for the rights of others, and they stand up for those who are marginalized and oppressed. They are champions for change.

- Educate yourself about social justice issues. The more you know about the challenges facing different communities, the better equipped you will be to speak out and take action. Find your voice. What are the issues that you are passionate about? What are the things that you can't stand to see? Once you know what you stand for, start speaking out. You can do this through social media, writing letters to the editor, or attending protests and rallies.

- Get involved in your community. Many organizations promote justice and equality. Find one that you care about and get involved. You can volunteer your time, donate money, or spread the word about their work. Be an ally. When you see someone being mistreated or discriminated against, speak up. Let them know that they are not alone and that you stand with them.

4. Be a good friend and family member. Warriors are often seen as fierce and fearless individuals fighting for their beliefs. But they are also more than that. Warriors are also kind, compassionate, and loving people who care deeply about the people in their lives. As a warrior, you have the power to make a real difference in the lives of the people you love. Be there for them when they need you.

One of the most important things you can do for your loved ones is be there when they need you. This doesn't mean you have to be physically present all the time. It simply means you are there to listen, offer support, and help however you can.

- Be supportive and encouraging. Everyone needs a cheerleader in their corner. As a warrior, you can be that cheerleader for your loved ones. Support their goals and dreams, even if they seem crazy or unrealistic. Encourage them to take risks and follow their passions.

- When your loved ones are feeling down, be there to pick them up. Remind them of their strengths and accomplishments. Help them to see the best in themselves.

- Help them achieve their goals and dreams. We all have goals and dreams in life, but sometimes, achieving them on our own can be hard. That's where you come in. As a warrior, you can help your loved ones achieve their goals and dreams. Whatever your loved one's goals and dreams are, help them to achieve them. Be their biggest supporter and their strongest advocate.

5. Live a life of integrity. Warriors are known for their honesty, integrity, and courage. They live their lives according to their values, even when it's difficult. Honesty is the foundation of your character. You are always truthful, even when it is difficult. You know that honesty is essential for building trust and respect. You also know that it is the only way to live a life that is true to yourself.

- Integrity is your guiding principle. You always act by your moral compass, even when it is inconvenient or unpopular. You are fair and just in your dealings with others. You keep your promises and honor your commitments.

- Courage is your greatest strength. You dare to face your fears and stand up for what is right, even when difficult. You are not afraid to challenge the status quo or fight for what you believe in.

As a warrior, you are called to live a life of purpose. You are responsible for using your gifts and talents to improve the world. You are a beacon of hope for the oppressed and downtrodden. You are a protector of the innocent and a defender of the weak.

6. Be a role model for others. Warriors are role models for others. They inspire others to be their best selves and to make a difference in the world.

To be a role model warrior, you must first live your life in a way that makes others want to be better people. This means being kind, compassionate, and respectful to everyone you meet, regardless of their background or beliefs. It also means being generous with your time and resources and always being willing to help others in need.

- Be honest and ethical in all of your dealings. Warriors are known for their integrity and their commitment to truth. When you are honest and ethical, you show others that it is possible to live a good life without compromising your values.

- Stand up for what is right, even when it is difficult. Warriors are not afraid to speak out against injustice and fight for their beliefs. When you stand up for what is right, you inspire others to do the same.

- Be forgiving and understanding. Everyone makes mistakes. As a role model warrior, you need to be forgiving and understanding of others. This doesn't mean that you have to condone bad behavior, but it does mean that you should be willing to give people second chances.

- Be humble and grateful. Warriors are often humble and grateful for the blessings in their lives. They know that they are not perfect, and they are always striving to improve. When you are humble and grateful, you show others that success is possible without being arrogant or entitled.

Inspiring Others to Be Warriors

Warriors inspire others to be warriors. They show others what is possible when they are willing to face their fears and overcome their obstacles. Warriors are not born. They are made. They are forged through the fires of adversity and the crucible of challenge.

If you want to inspire others to be warriors, you must first be a warrior yourself. You must develop a warrior mindset. This means cultivating courage, resilience, and perseverance. It means learning to embrace challenges and setbacks as opportunities for growth.

Here are some ways to develop a warrior mindset:

1. Identify your values. What is important to you? What are you willing to fight for? Once you know your values, you can start to live in alignment with them. This will give you a sense of purpose and direction, which are essential for developing a warrior mindset.

2. Face your fears. Everyone has fears, but warriors don't let them control them. They face their fears head-on, knowing that the only way to overcome them is to confront them.

3. Develop resilience. Resilience is the ability to bounce back from setbacks and adversity. Warriors are resilient. They don't give up easily. They learn from their mistakes and keep moving forward.

4. Embrace challenges. Warriors see challenges as opportunities to learn and grow. They don't shy away from challenges. They embrace them with courage and determination.

5. Be persistent. Perseverance is the key to success. Warriors never give up. They keep going even when things are tough. They know that the only way to achieve their goals is to persevere.

How can you inspire others to be warriors?

- **Be authentic.** People can spot a fake from a mile away. Be yourself and share your true story. Be honest about your challenges and your triumphs. This will help others connect with you deeper and see that they are not alone.

- **Be vulnerable.** It takes courage to be vulnerable, but it is essential for inspiring others. When you share your vulnerabilities, you show others that it is okay to be imperfect. You also give them permission to be themselves and share their stories.

- **Be positive.** Warriors are positive people. They have a positive attitude, even in the face of adversity. They believe in themselves and in their ability to overcome any challenge. When you are positive, you inspire others to be positive as well.

- **Be compassionate.** Warriors are compassionate people. They care about others and want to help them succeed. They are willing to share their knowledge and experience with others. When you are compassionate, you inspire others to be compassionate as well.

- **Lead by example.** The best way to inspire others is to lead by example. Show others what it means to be a warrior. Be courageous, be resilient, and be persistent. When you live a warrior's life, you inspire others to do the same.

Share Your Story

One of the best ways to inspire others to be warriors is to share your story. How did you develop a warrior mindset? What challenges did you overcome? What lessons did you learn along the way?

Your story can be a powerful source of inspiration for others. It can show them that it is possible to overcome any obstacle, no matter how difficult it may seem.

When sharing your story, be honest and open. Don't shy away from the challenges you faced or the mistakes you made. Your story will be more inspiring if it is authentic and relatable.

Be a Mentor

Another great way to inspire others to be warriors is to be a mentor. If you know someone trying to develop a warrior mindset, offer them your guidance and support.

Share your insights and knowledge with them. Help them to identify and overcome their challenges. Be there when they need someone to talk to or lean on. Being a mentor can be a rewarding experience. It is an opportunity to make a real difference in someone's life.

Create Content

You can inspire others to be warriors by creating content like blog posts, articles, or videos. Share your insights and knowledge on the warrior mindset and personal development. Your content can help others to learn about the warrior mindset and how to develop it. It can also help them to overcome their challenges and achieve their goals.

When creating content, focus on providing value to your readers or viewers. Share your own experiences and lessons learned. Be genuine and authentic.

Creating a Lasting Legacy

Warriors create lasting legacies. They leave behind a world that is better than they found it. They are not afraid to stand up for what is right, even when difficult. They are willing to fight for what they believe in and never give up on their dreams.

If you want to create a lasting legacy, you must live like a warrior. You need to be courageous, compassionate and committed to making a difference in the world. Here are a few tips:

1. Find your cause. What are you passionate about? What problem do you want to solve? What need do you want to meet? Once you know your cause, you can start developing a plan to make a difference.

2. Be willing to take risks. Warriors are not afraid to take risks. They know there is no guarantee of success, but they are willing to put themselves out there and give it their all. If you want to create a lasting legacy, you need to be willing to step outside of your comfort zone and take risks.

3. Be persistent. Warriors never give up. They are persistent in pursuing their goals, even when faced with setbacks and challenges. If you want to create a lasting legacy, you need to be persistent and never give up on your dreams.

4. Inspire others. Warriors inspire others to be the best versions of themselves. They share their knowledge and insights and encourage others to follow their dreams. If you want to create a lasting legacy, you need to inspire others to make a difference in the world.

Here are some specific examples of how you can create a lasting legacy as a warrior:

1. Start a business or organization to impact the world positively. There are many problems in the world that need to be solved. If you have an idea for a business or organization that can make a difference, go for it! Even if your business doesn't become the next Google, you can still positively impact the world.

Here are a few examples of businesses and organizations that are making a positive impact on the world:

- Tesla is working to reduce our reliance on fossil fuels and create a more sustainable future.

- Khan Academy provides free, high-quality education to people all over the world.

- Water.org is working to ensure that everyone has access to clean water.

2. Write a book or create a piece of art that inspires others. If you have a story or a message to share, write a book or create a piece of art. Your work could inspire others to follow their dreams, make a difference, or see the world differently. Here are a few examples of books and pieces of art that have inspired people all over the world:

- The Alchemist by Paulo Coelho is a novel about following your dreams.

- The Mona Lisa by Leonardo da Vinci is a painting that has inspired people for centuries.

- Imagine by John Lennon is a song that inspires people to dream of a better world.

3. Raise your children to be warriors. Teach your children the values of integrity, honor, respect, courage, and compassion. Help them to develop a warrior mindset. When you raise your children to be warriors, you create a lasting legacy that will continue beyond your lifetime. Here are a few tips on how to raise your children to be warriors:

- Teach them to stand up for what is right, even when difficult.

- Encourage them to take risks and pursue their dreams.

- Help them to develop a strong sense of self-worth and self-confidence.

- Teach them the importance of hard work and perseverance.

- Model the behavior that you want to see in them.

Creating a lasting legacy is not easy. It takes hard work, dedication, and courage. But if you are willing to put in the effort, you can make a difference in the world and leave behind a legacy that will last for generations to come.

Chapter 12:
The Warrior's
Mindset in Action

H ave you ever wondered what it takes to be a warrior? Warriors are not just people who fight in wars. Warriors are people who have developed a mindset that allows them to overcome any challenge and achieve their goals.

In this chapter, we will explore the warrior mindset in action. We will examine case studies of warriors in business and life, learn lessons from warrior leaders, and discuss how to apply the warrior mindset to one's own life.

Case Studies of Warriors in Business and Life

Imagine yourself in Oprah Winfrey's shoes. You were born into poverty and abuse, but you never gave up on yourself or your dreams. You worked hard and overcame all the challenges in your life. You became one of the most successful women in the world, inspiring many. You are a warrior.

Imagine yourself in the shoes of Steve Jobs. You were fired from your own company, but you started another company and revolutionized the animation industry. You then returned to your first company and led it to unprecedented success. You never gave up on your vision, even when things were tough. You are a warrior.

Imagine yourself in Nelson Mandela's shoes. You spent 27 years in prison for fighting for what you believed in. After your release, you became the first black president of your country and led it to reconciliation and peace. You are a warrior.

What do these three people have in common? They are all warriors. They have all overcome challenges, faced adversity, and never given up on their dreams. They are all an inspiration to us all.

These are just a few examples of warriors in business and life. Many others have faced challenges and adversity but never gave up on their dreams. These people inspire us all.

Lessons from Warrior Leaders

Warrior leaders are some of the most inspiring and successful people in history. They have faced incredible challenges and overcome seemingly impossible odds. But what makes warrior leaders so special?

One of the most important qualities of a warrior leader is a clear vision. Warriors know what they want to achieve and are laser-focused on achieving it. For example, Alexander the Great had a vision to conquer the known world and never gave up on his dream. Despite facing numerous setbacks, he eventually achieved his goal and became one of the most successful conquerors in history.

Another essential quality of a warrior leader is courage. Warriors are not afraid to take risks and face their fears. They know that courage is essential for success. For example, Queen Boudicca of the Iceni led her people in a rebellion against the Romans, even though she knew she was outnumbered and outgunned. Her courage and determination inspired her people, who inflicted heavy casualties on the Romans.

Warrior leaders are also persistent. They never give up on their dreams, even in adversity. For example, Mahatma Gandhi led the Indian independence movement for over two decades, even though he was repeatedly jailed and beaten by the British authorities. His persistence and dedication eventually paid off, and India gained independence in 1947.

In addition to courage and determination, warrior leaders are also compassionate. They care about others, and they strive to make the world a better place. They use their strength and power to help others. For example, Nelson Mandela fought against apartheid in South Africa, and after he was elected president, he worked to reconcile the black and white communities. His compassion and forgiveness helped to heal the divisions in South African society.

How can you apply the lessons of warrior leaders to your life?

Even if you are not a warrior in the traditional sense, you can still learn from the lessons of warrior leaders. Here are a few tips:

- **Have a clear vision.** What do you want to achieve in your life? Once you know what you want, develop a plan to achieve it. Break down your goals into smaller, more manageable steps and set deadlines for yourself.

- **Be courageous.** Take risks and step outside of your comfort zone. Don't be afraid to fail. Failure is a part of the learning process. The important thing is to pick yourself up and keep moving forward.

- **Be persistent.** Never give up on your dreams, even when things are tough. Keep working towards your goals, even when you face setbacks. Remember, the only way to fail is to give up.

- **Be compassionate.** Care about others and help them whenever you can. Use your strengths and talents to make the world a better place.

Conclusion

I n today's fast-paced and ever-changing world, cultivating a fearless warrior mindset is more important than ever. This mindset is not just about being tough or physically strong; it's about embracing challenges, overcoming obstacles, and living with unwavering courage.

The warrior mindset is not reserved for a select few; it's a birthright we all possess, waiting to be awakened. By understanding and embodying the principles of the warrior mindset, we can empower ourselves to live our best lives and positively impact the world around us.

At the core of the warrior mindset is courage. Courage is not the absence of fear but the triumph over it. It's about acknowledging our fears, confronting them head-on, and transforming them into sources of strength. When we embrace our fears, we no longer have to let them control us. We can become more resilient and adaptable in the face of adversity. We can also learn to take calculated risks and pursue our dreams with greater determination.

Another essential pillar of the warrior mindset is resilience. Resilience is the ability to bounce back from setbacks and challenges. It's about grit and perseverance, even when things get tough.

Resilient warriors understand that setbacks are a normal part of life. They don't allow failures to define them or derail their progress. Instead, they learn from their mistakes, grow stronger, and emerge wiser and more determined from challenges.

The warrior mindset is also grounded in a growth mindset. This is the belief that we can all learn and grow regardless of age, background, or circumstances.

Warriors embrace challenges as opportunities to learn and grow. They are unafraid to step outside their comfort zone and try new things. They also seek feedback and mentorship from others who can help them reach their full potential.

The warrior mindset recognizes the importance of integrating physical and mental disciplines. A healthy body fosters a resilient mind, and vice versa.

Warriors care for their physical health by eating nutritious foods, exercising regularly, and getting enough sleep. They also cultivate their mental well-being through meditation, yoga, and journaling. Warriors become more balanced and centered individuals by integrating physical and mental disciplines. They can better manage stress, navigate challenges, and perform at their peak.

The warrior mindset is not a new concept. It has been cultivated and refined by warriors throughout history. Today, we can still learn valuable lessons from the wisdom of ancient warriors. By applying these principles to our lives, we can develop the courage, resilience, and discipline necessary to thrive in the modern world.

For example, the Taoist sage Lao Tzu taught that "the greatest victory is that which requires no battle." This principle reminds us that the best way to overcome our adversaries is to understand them and to find common ground.

Another ancient warrior principle is that "the true enemy is within." This principle teaches us that our greatest challenges come not from external forces but from our minds and emotions. By conquering our inner demons, we become more powerful and unstoppable.

The warrior mindset is not just about strength and courage; it's also about ethical leadership. Warriors lead with integrity, honesty, and accountability. They are committed to serving others and positively impacting the world. Ethical warriors are humble and compassionate. They use their power and influence to lift others and to create a more just and equitable world.

Throughout history, we have seen the transformative impact of fearless leaders. These leaders have inspired us with courage, resilience, and ethical leadership. Nelson Mandela, Martin Luther King, Jr., and Mother Teresa are just a few fearless leaders who have left an indelible mark on the world. Their stories remind us that even one person can make a difference.

Now is the time to embrace your warrior path. The world needs your courage, resilience, and ethical leadership. By embodying the principles of the warrior mindset, you can create a better life for yourself and those around you. You can also inspire others to live their lives to the fullest and positively impact the world.

Sticking to your values may shake things up. Ignoring appearances might sometimes lead to being left out. Letting go of stuff could leave you feeling broke now and then. But if you truly know yourself, your goals, and your principles, you'll know what's right and have the guts to do it. And that means being okay with whatever comes next.

Here's the big lesson: be ready to face reality. Be bold, take risks, and handle the criticism like a champ. It's all about the lessons from stoicism, minimalism, and facing fears we've talked about before. They're super important.

When you accept that mistakes happen and learn from them, you'll become more sure of yourself and get things done faster. People scared to mess up or upset others can't make decisions. But not you. You're a warrior, walking your path and owning the consequences like a grown-up.

You ask for forgiveness, not permission. And if you don't get it, keep going anyway, knowing you did what's right for you because you're a warrior.

Made in the USA
Columbia, SC
16 July 2024